THE ORDINATION OF WOMEN TO THE PRIESTHOOD

A SECOND REPORT BY THE HOUSE OF BISHOPS

GS 82ᴾ

General Synod of the Church of England
Church House, Great Smith Street, London SW1P 3NZ

3721 2

blished June 1988 by the General Synod of the Church of England

The First Report, to which this is a sequel, is GS 764. The
Ordination of Women to the Priesthood: A Report by the House of
Bishops.

The draft legislation is contained in GS 830-33

All the above are available from Church House Bookshop, 31 Great
Smith Street, London SW1P 3BN.

Contents

PREFACE

Preface

The House of Bishops, in its first Report (GS 764) to the General
Synod in February 1987, undertook to continue to reflect upon the
theological issues arising from the question of the ordination of
Women to the Priesthood and to report further to the General Synod
upon those issues.

This second Report from the House is the fruit of that process of
continued theological reflection.

In considering this Report the House of Bishops hopes the General
Synod and wider Church will bear three things in mind:

First, the carefully expressed common convictions which all
members of the House share. The differing judgements of members
of the House on the ordination of women to the priesthood have
been set in a framework of shared belief which must not be
underestimated.

Second, the Bishops have listened patiently to each other's
strongly held convictions. They have learnt much from each other
and respect each other's integrity. The House has worked
carefully to give fair and precise expression to the various
points of view represented among its membership. The House
believes that the Report accurately articulates these positions
and its Report is unanimous. It therefore has reason to hope that
others may also be able to recognize their convictions within the
Report.

Third, the Bishops hope that something of the manner and precision
of their theological debate will also inform the deliberations of
the Synod and wider Church as the Church of England comes to make
an actual decision on the ordination of women to the priesthood on
the basis of the separate legislative proposals about to be put
before the Church.

On behalf of the House of Bishops

Robert Cantuar:

Chairman

May, 1988

Chapter 1

INTRODUCTION

(i) Background to this Report

1 The debate on the ordination of women to the priesthood within the Church of England, the Anglican Communion and within the wider ecumenical movement has a long history. The immediate background to this Report lies in the moves to draw up legislation to enable women to be ordained priest in the Church of England. At the July 1986 Group of Sessions the General Synod debated the Report The Ordination of Women to the Priesthood: The Scope of the Legislation, GS 738. In view of the anxiety felt by many at some of the options put forward in the McClean Report the General Synod agreed an amendment, moved on behalf of the House of Bishops by the Archbishop of York, to the effect that further consideration of the Report be postponed 'to enable the House of Bishops to report to the Synod before steps are taken to prepare legislation, the Bishops' Report to be presented not later than February, 1987'.

2 The House of Bishops duly presented their Report on the legislation to the General Synod in February 1987, The Ordination of Women to the Priesthood: A Report by the House of Bishops, GS 764. That Report sought to identify the principal theological issues involved in proceeding to ordain women; set out principles on which any legislation should be based; and gave a detailed framework for legislation and for safeguards in the event of the Church of England deciding to go ahead and ordain women to the priesthood.

1

3 The Report of the House of Bishops was welcomed by the General Synod. A motion was passed requesting the Standing Committee of the General Synod, in bringing forward legislation to authorise the ordination of women to the priesthood, to do so in accordance with the guidelines in the Report. At the same time the House of Bishops promised to continue to reflect on the theological issues. The bishops hoped that by encouraging widespread debate of the issues a greater measure of clarity about the underlying theological principles would emerge. In a subsequent note to the General Synod in July 1987 the House of Bishops expressed its intention of presenting its theological reflections to the Synod alongside the presentation of the legislation itself.

4 The decision of the bishops to undertake theological reflection was not intended to deny the important debate that has already taken place within the Church of England. A valuable contribution to the discussion of the theological issues is in the Reports prepared by Dame Christian Howard as well as in the contributions offered by Synod members in the course of the earlier debates (1). However, the bishops believe it important, as the Church of England draws up legislation, to set out the degree of theological agreement that exists amongst themselves and to identify the specific issues where disagreement remains.

5 This Report was prepared by a group made up of seven bishops and four consultants (three of them women). The group explored the question of the ordination of women to the priesthood in an atmosphere of openness and trust, recognising that the issues raised in the debate touch us all deeply and involve not only what we think but what we feel. Members of the group were helped to understand why they held their particular views and also to recognise the integrity of those whose views differ from their own. The group hopes that what it experienced in its discussions

2

will be experienced by many others as they engage in the debate.

6   The House of Bishops commented upon this Report at various stages in its development. Not every member of the House would want to express the matter in precisely the way it is expressed here; nevertheless, **the House presents this Report as its Report.** The bishops consider that the crucial issues have been identified and that the different opinions held on those issues are fairly represented. As the General Synod invited the bishops to guide them in this debate, the final chapter of this Report sets out the range of opinions that exists in the House on whether it is right for the Church of England to proceed in this matter, whether it should proceed now, or whether it should exercise restraint. We have tried also to indicate where the weight of opinion lies.

(ii) Ten Years of Debate in the Church of England

7   In 1973 two motions were considered by the General Synod and subsequently referred to the dioceses. In 1975 the Synod returned to the motions. The first motion before the Synod was:

> that this Synod considers that there are no fundamental objections to the ordination of women to the priesthood.

This was carried as follows:

	Ayes	Noes	Abstentions
House of Bishops	28	10	0
House of Clergy	110	96	2
House of Laity	117	74	3

A second motion 'that this Synod considers that the Church of England should now proceed to remove the legal and other barriers to the ordination of women' was not put to the Synod because of the divided nature of the voting in diocesan synods. In its place the Synod voted on the motion:

3

that this Synod, in view of the significant division of
opinion reflected in the diocesan voting, considers that
it would not be right at present to remove the legal and
other barriers to the ordination of women.
The voting on this motion was:

	Ayes	Noes	Abstentions
House of Bishops	19	14	1
House of Clergy	127	74	0
House of Laity	80	96	0

8   In 1978 the Synod voted on the motion:

that this Synod asks the Standing Committee to prepare
and bring forward legislation to remove the barriers to
the ordination of women to the priesthood and their
consecration to the episcopate.

The motion was lost in the House of Clergy.

	Ayes	Noes
House of Bishops	32	17
House of Clergy	94	149
House of Laity	120	106
	Abstentions	3

9   In November 1984 a motion urging the drawing up of legislation
came to the Synod by way of diocesan synod motions:

that this Synod calls the Standing Committee to bring
forward legislation to permit the ordination of women to
the priesthood in the Provinces of Canterbury and York.

This motion was passed in all three Houses.

	Ayes	Noes
House of Bishops	41	6
House of Clergy	131	98
House of Laity	138	79
	Abstentions	5

10   In February 1987 the House of Bishops presented its Report
setting out the principles on which legislation should be based.
The motion before the Synod, put by the Archbishop of Canterbury,
was:

4

that this Synod, welcoming the Report (GS 764) from the House of Bishops instructs:

(a) the Standing Committee of the General Synod in bring forward legislation to authorise the ordination of women to the priesthood to do so in accordance with the guidelines in the Report: and

(b) the House of Bishops to begin to prepare the Code of Practice envisaged in the Report.

The voting was as follows:

	Ayes	Noes
House of Bishops	32	8
House of Clergy	135	70
House of Laity	156	67
	Abstentions	2

11   The voting figures on these motions would seem, therefore, to suggest that the majority of the bishops in the House of Bishops have in the past favoured the ordination of women. It is possible that some bishops who voted in February, 1987 for the drawing up of legislation will not vote for that legislation when it comes before the Synod. Some of those bishops may have regarded the drawing up of specific legislation as a way of bringing to the attention of the Church of England the real threat to the unity of the Church of England which such legislation might involve. Neither the Group responsible for drafting this Report, nor the House of Bishops as a whole, has, during the formulation of this Report, had knowledge of the proposed legislation.

12   The General Synod has in the last ten years also considered related issues which support the view that the majority of bishops favours women's ordination. There was a clear majority in the House in favour of allowing women lawfully ordained abroad to preside at the eucharist in this country. And the vote on the motion relating to the English Covenant Proposals accepting 'provisions for the recognition and acceptance of women's

ministries of the other Covenanting Churches as presbyters', a
motion which failed in the House of Clergy, was 37 votes in
favour and 9 against in the House of Bishops.

13   In referring to these voting figures on motions relating to
the ordination of women to the priesthood, we are not meaning to
imply that the past voting pattern of the House of Bishops should,
or will, determine the outcome of this present debate. Neither are
we suggesting that a matter as crucial as the ordination of women
should be settled by bare synodical majorities in isolation from
the testing and forming of the mind of the Church. Indeed, this
is precisely why we have undertaken to guide the Church of England
in a period of prayerful reflection on the theological issues. We
are anxious that any synodical decision and subsequent action
should reflect a carefully and widely formed mind of the Church.
And, even after a synodical decision has been expressed, that
decision has to be received in the life of the people of God.
Reception has to go on in the Anglican Communion and in the other
churches, both those which have retained the catholic order and
those who have not. Only if it is so received can a decision
by a single Province, or by several Provinces, be deemed to be the
mind of Christ. We believe that one of the ways the House of
Bishops can and should serve the Church is by giving a lead in the
process of forming the mind of the Church. This Report is written
for that purpose. The House will continue to listen carefully to
the views which are expressed in the General Synod and more widely
in the Church.

(iii) Some Themes which Underlie the Debate

14   In forming a mind on whether women should or should not be
ordained to a priestly ministry, judgements have to be made in the
area of God's revelation in creation, history and in the

6

particularity of the incarnation; the authority of Scripture, tradition, reason and experience; the nature and purpose of the Church; how the Church comes to make decisions on matters of faith and order; the priesthood of the ordained ministry; the nature of men and women created in God's image; the evaluation of cultural difference; and the sexual dimension in the exercise of ministry. Each of these areas inter-relates with others and contains within itself a number of interlocking issues. Important features of the discussion are its complexity, the close inter-relationship of the issues, and the varying weight those issues carry in the minds of those who are trying to form an overall judgement. The view a person takes, for example, of Scripture and tradition, or of the representative character of the priesthood of the ordained ministry, will to a large extent determine the relevance or not of other issues and be decisive in the overall judgement made. So also will the view taken on how authoritative decisions on the ministry can be taken.

15   As we explored the issues taken up in the chapters of this Report we discovered that there were certain themes underlying the arguments to which we kept returning. In particular we needed to clarify the sense in which we were using the term priest. A second area in which misunderstanding easily arose amongst us was our understanding of the significance of the distinction between male-female and masculine-feminine. A third matter to be faced was the status of the question of the ordination of women: how important is it and in what respects? A further area constantly at issue was how we use the sources of Christian authority, Scripture, tradition, reason and experience, in forming our mind on matters of faith and order. Related to this is how decisions are made when there is division in the universal Church.

16   In the paragraphs that follow we set out some of our thinking
on four of these issues. These explorations are intended to help
the reader through the arguments of Chapters 2 - 4. In Chapter 5
we return to reflect at some length on how we have used the
sources of Christian authority. Finally, in Chapter 6 we take up
the question of decision making when there is division in the
Church.

(a) The priesthood of the ordained ministry

17   The title of our Report, The Ordination of Women to the
Priesthood uses the terminology of our earlier Report (GS 764)
both on the grounds of consistency of use, and because the
parallel Report on legislation of necessity uses this terminology.
We recognise that the understanding of priesthood within the
Church of England and within the Anglican Communion is the subject
of continuing reflection. This is an important part of the
context in which the Church of England is being asked to make a
decision on the ordination of women to the priesthood. Whatever
the differences of understanding between us we all affirm the
teaching of the Church as it is set out in the Ordinal and the
Book of Common Prayer. The Bishop describes those to be ordained
priest as being called 'to be messengers, watchmen, and stewards of
the Lord; to teach and to premonish, to feed and provide for the
Lord's family; to seek for Christ's sheep that are dispersed
abroad...' When the Bishop lays his hands on the head of the
ordinand he prays:

> Receive the Holy Ghost for the office and work of a
> Priest in the Church of God, now committed unto thee by
> the imposition of our hands. Whose sins thou dost
> forgive, they are forgiven; and whose sins thou dost
> retain, they are retained. And be thou a faithful
> dispenser of the Word of God, and of his holy Sacraments;
> In the Name of the Father, and of the Son, and of the
> Holy Ghost. Amen.

8

And in giving the Bible the Bishop says:

> Take thou authority to preach the Word of God, and to
> minister the holy Sacraments in the Congregation, where
> thou shalt be lawfully appointed thereunto.

18   In the service for the Ordination of Priests in the
Alternative Service Book the Bishop describes the ministry of
those to be ordained in the following way:

> A priest is called by God to work with the bishop and
> with his fellow-priests, as servant and shepherd among
> the people to whom he is sent. He is to proclaim the
> word of the Lord, to call his hearers to repentance, and
> in Christ's name to absolve, and declare the forgiveness
> of sins. He is to baptise, and to prepare the baptised
> for Confirmation. He is to preside at the celebration of
> the Holy Communion. He is to lead his people in prayer
> and worship, to intercede for them, to bless them in the
> name of the Lord, and to teach and encourage by word and
> example. He is to minister to the sick, and prepare the
> dying for their death. He must set the Good Shepherd
> always before him as the pattern of his calling, caring
> for the people committed to his charge, and joining with
> them in a common witness to the world.

19   The words of the Book of Common Prayer and the Alternative
Service Book lead us to affirm together that the ministry to which
priests are ordained is a ministry of Word and Sacraments, of
oversight and pastoral care. It is a ministry given by Christ to
those called by God within the Church to that ministry. This
priestly ministry is focussed in the ministry of Word and
Sacrament, through which the Holy Spirit makes Christ's
reconciling presence among his people known and in response to
which the people are enabled to offer to God the sacrifice of
themselves, in, with and through Christ, in worship and in lives
of service and witness in the world. The ministry of presbyters
can be called priestly in that it is their vocation to help the
people of God to realise their priestly vocation in the world.

20 Women now ordained deacons already exercise a representative ministry of the Word; they also administer the sacrament of baptism and solemnise marriage; exercise pastoral care and take a lead in mission. It is not sufficient to argue that because women are now, as deacons, within Holy Orders the other two orders should be open to them. The ordination of women to the priesthood raises further matters. These relate particularly to a ministry of oversight and leadership of the people of God and a ministry which, in a particular way (though not exclusively), is focussed in the presidency of the eucharist, the celebration of which makes present sacramentally the fruits of Christ's once-for-all sacrifice and his continuing High Priesthood. Is it appropriate for women to be ordained to a ministry of priesthood with these characteristic functions and with such symbolism as reveals the nature of this ministry? This is a question to which we return in Chapter 2.

(b) Male and female, masculine and feminine

21 In discussing the Genesis text 'male and female created he them', the meaning of the particularity of maleness in the incarnation, and the representative function of the priest we found ourselves questioning one another about how we understand the nature of men and women and those qualities which we designate as 'masculine' and 'feminine'. Sex differences are invoked on both sides of the debate on the ordination of women.

22 The most obvious characteristic of the human race, indeed of all developed organisms, is the differentiation of sex. Every man or women owes his or her existence and individuality to the differences between the sexes and to the relationship between them. For the Christian whose faith is rooted in belief in God

10

who created all things and 'behold, they were very good', this difference is to be welcomed. In Christ it is not to be abolished in this world but is enabled to be the means by which it can become an expression of the love of God himself. It is, therefore, not to be minimised or denied, as if it were an undesirable or regrettable characteristic of humankind.

23   Every individual inherits both male and female tendencies: sex is determined by the tilting of the balance one way or another. There are recognised and recognisable anatomical and physiological differences between male and females other than those concerned with primary and secondary sexual characteristics and with conception and childbirth. There is a specific genetic differentation in that a man possesses a 'Y' chromosome which a woman does not. Males are generally taller and stronger than females: females generally develop more quickly. But some women are taller than some men and some men develop more quickly than some women.

24   Psychological differences are, however, much more difficult to assess. Some physical factors undoubtedly have a direct psychological effect. Some basic psychological differences are to be associated with genetic, anatomical and physiological differences. Male and female sex hormones do influence certain aspects of behaviour like aggressiveness or gentleness. But, as each sex secretes both types of hormones, the difference can only be one of degree and will vary with the individual man and the individual woman. Many psychologists today, though not all, argue that the differences are much less pronounced than is sometimes argued:

> I do not think that we can as yet say what 'masculinity'
> or 'femininity' really mean. All we know is what has

11

traditionally been seen as masculine and feminine: that
there is a traditional agreement on what are feminine
personality attributes (i.e. affectionate, warm,
dependent, sensitive, caring etc.) and what are masculine
attributes (i.e. independent, assertive, dominant,
competitive, forceful etc. (2).

Whether differences are effected by cultural conditioning to a
greater extent than determined by innate difference is much
debated. From an early age boys and girls are subject to
different environmental influences and respond to stereotypical
patterns expected of them.

25   While there are accepted biological, physiological and
psychological differences between males and females and an
interconnection between them, the differences may not always be as
clear or as marked as sometimes was held in the past. Moreover,
those differences can be reinforced or minimised by cultural
factors. Further, different cultures set different values on
masculine and feminine traits. This may lead to a man being
forced to renounce qualities regarded as feminine and a woman
those qualities regarded as masculine. In such a way an
intolerable strain is put on individuals which limits the potential
and growth of the individual.

26   Our personal perception and estimation of sexual
differentiation clearly affects the debate on the ordination of
women. Further, phrases like 'the essential nature of man' and
'the essential nature of woman' need to be constantly questioned.
Each of us tends to imagine that the view held by us on sexual
differentiation at this particular moment is true, always was so
and always will be. Yet a review of different periods in history,
of different cultures as well as the views of contemporary
scientists, would suggest that we all need to ask questions about

12

the particular assumptions we bring to the subject. There are those of us who consider that the differences between the sexes, and the appropriation of certain characteristics for men and other characteristics for women, are of primary significance about our common humanity. Others of us, however, tend to believe that more significant than the differences between the sexes is the fact that women and men are human beings sharing a basic human nature, and sharing the same potentialities, desires and fears. Among those who hold the former view are to be found those who believe that only men should be priests and that women have other, complementary ministries. Among those who hold the latter view are to be found those who believe that it is appropriate that both men and women should be ordained.

27 A closely related factor in the debate on the ordination of women is the significance of the symbolism of sexual difference and of the duality of masculine and feminine. Throughout history the perceived differences between the sexes have undoubtedly been seen as possessing a deep significance for human existence. Sexual symbolism has been, and still is, powerful in theology as well as in the liturgical and devotional life of the Christian community. Symbols are an essential element in religious language and culture and help to maintain and hold together the structure of communities; therefore it is threatening and dangerous to change religious symbols. It is not surprising that for some the important question is therefore not whether a woman in fact has the capacities to perform all the duties of a priest; clearly many women do possess remarkable gifts, as do many men, for pastoral care, for mission and for proclaiming and teaching the Word. Nevertheless this does not answer the question what a woman would symbolise to those in her care and, in particular, what she would symbolise in the liturgy of the eucharist. There would be

then, for some people, a distortion of the truth if the symbolism
of an all male priesthood were to be changed.

28   The masculine and feminine have been and.still are for many
associated with particular approaches to the meaning of life and
its fulfilment. The masculine and feminine are not merely
expressions of psychological differences between individuals.
They express both the nature of reality and our attitude to it.
Some of us consider that the duality between masculine and
feminine is the highest expression of that duality which runs
through the whole of creation and which is expressed in, for
example, positive and negative charges, energy and inertia, major
and minor chords, the active and the passive, give and take,
initiative and response. The energy and impetus for life in all
its aspects springs from the creative tension of that dialectic.

29   There are those of us who believe that in the case of human
beings the difference between the sexes is not merely biological
or cultural but also symbolic. It is the symbolism attached to
the difference which is of such power in affecting our
understanding of God and his relationship to creation and to
humankind. This power can be consecrated only if the dialectic is
recognised and its potential faced.

30   Some of the disagreements which exist over the ordination of
women to the priesthood lie in the area of the extent to which the
dialectic and its symbolism is reflected and embodied in the fact
that it was male human nature that the Word of God united to his
divine nature, but it was female human nature that was chosen to
be the bearer of the eternal Word of God (cf para. 57).
31   Others of us, while not wanting to minimise the power of
symbols in religious language and ritual, are aware that symbols

14

may lose their power with social change: they may come to convey a message no longer consonant with our understanding of the Christian Gospel. It has therefore to be asked whether a particular symbol says to the Church and the world what is still believed. It maybe that a symbol comes to reinforce patterns of inequality and fosters a sense of alienation, making it hard for the Church to be seen as a community of reconciliation. An inherited symbol may come to deny what as Christians we believe about the basic unity of human nature and the richness and variety of complementarity. On the other hand it may be necessary for the Church to retain and use certain symbols, precisely because they express revealed truths by which the world is judged.

32   The question of symbolism as it relates to male-female, masculine-feminine, in the ordination of women debate is a complex but significant one. We return to the question in Chapter 2.

(c) The status of the question

33   As we considered the arguments for and against the ordination of women we found ourselves asking, what is the status of the question of the ordination of women to the priesthood? It is sometimes argued that this is a 'second order' question, such as obligatory clerical celibacy, not impinging directly upon 'first order' questions, such as the doctrine of the Trinity, or of the Person of Christ, or of the Atonement, where the central tenets of the Christian faith are plainly at stake. However, we have come to doubt whether in this context such a distinction is useful. This for two reasons:
(a) For many of those who favour the ordination of women, as
     well as for many of those who do not, the question is not
     one of comparative doctrinal indifference. It is seen as
     closely bound up with what is believed about the nature

15

of God, about Christ and about the Church and about creation. It is thus intimately related to the 'centre' of the faith.

(b) The distinction is also unhelpful insofar as it may appear to imply a distinction between matters of faith as primary and matters of order as secondary. But it is an article of faith that the Church is a communion of saints. The ordained ministry is a principal instrument given by God for the maintenance of true communion. In this way questions of church order touch upon matters of faith.

(d) Sources of Authority

34   In the Church of England it is generally agreed that the sources of authority are Scripture, tradition and reason. Whilst the Scriptures are our primary and normative source, possessing 'controlling authority', we have further appealed to tradition and reason when reflecting upon, and deciding about, questions of faith, order and morals. Scripture has its own cultural context, as do the creeds and the continuing tradition and experience of the Church. The hermeneutical task is to attempt to discern on the one hand what is abiding and continuing truth, and on the other what belongs to the particular place and time. It is this abiding and continuing truth which needs to be re-expressed and lived in today's world. We have considered the evidence of Scripture and tradition in exploring the question of priesthood and the representation of Christ (Chapter 2) and priesthood, headship and authority (Chapter 3). Although we all accept the 'controlling authority' of Scripture and the authority of the Church's tradition, we soon discovered that we differed in our interpretation of those sources. These differences lead us to different conclusions about whether women should or should not be ordained as priests. We have taken this up in greater detail in Chapter 5.

35   We hope that what we have said about these four themes will help the readers follow the arguments in the rest of our Report.

(iv) Identifying the Issues in the Current Debate

36   A vast amount has been written on the subject of the ordination of women by Anglicans and by those from other traditions, by theologians, sociologists and anthropologists, by ordained and unordained, by women and men, by proponents and opponents of the ordination of women. We do not intend in this report to produce a comprehensive review of all the arguments for and against but rather to concentrate on those central issues in the current debate on which we are divided amongst ourselves. These issues have already been highlighted in Christian Howard's Report The Ordination of Women to the Priesthood: Further Report, GS Misc 198; by the Faith and Order Advisory Group in The Priesthood of the Ordained Ministry, GS 694; and in the recent correspondence between the Archbishop of Canterbury, the Pope and Cardinal Willebrands (cf Appendix). In our own discussions we have found that those are the issues to which we have returned again and again.

37   **Five issues** have been identified as particularly relevant in the present debate:
- the ordained priest has a representative function, both in representing Christ to the people and the people to God. Can such a function be appropriately exercised by women as well as men? This involves considering what significance is to be placed on the maleness of Jesus and whether it is therefore appropriate for women to represent Christ to the people. It also raises questions concerning the significance of male and female in the order of creation and whether women can represent the whole Church before God as men have traditionally done.

17

- texts in 1 Corinthians and 1 Timothy speak of the subordination of women to men and man as the head of woman. What implications has this for the exercise of a priestly ministry which is to lead the community and exercise authority in the community?

- one function of ordination is to show beyond doubt that the person so ordained has authority to act on behalf of the community. Is it possible while the Church remains divided upon the question of the ordination of women to the priesthood that women can be recognised as able to exercise authority on behalf of the whole Church?

- Anglicans use Scripture, tradition and reason in coming to decisions about matters of faith and order in the Church. More and more women in the accredited lay ministry are claiming a vocation to a priestly ministry. Moreover, congregations are affirming that call and asking the Church to test their call. What questions does such contemporary experience pose in respect of the tradition of the Church?

- the Church has two thousand years of unbroken tradition of a male priesthood. In view of the fact that Anglicans claim to have a ministry within the universal Church can such a change in the tradition be made without the authority of a truly ecumenical council?

38　The first of these issues was underlined in our own earlier Report, GS 764.

One issue of particular significance in the current discussion is that of the representative character of the priesthood of the ordained ministry as is illustrated in the correspondence between the Archbishop of Canterbury and Cardinal Willebrands (GS Misc 245). At issue is the representative character of the priestly ministry, both in representing Christ to the people and in representing the people through Christ to the Father. Can the presence of Christ be appropriately represented by a woman priest, and can the people be appropriately represented if women are excluded from the priesthood? Is there any theological significance in the maleness of Jesus and, if so, how is this related to the human nature of the ascended Christ in whom, as our High Priest, the whole of redeemed humanity is presented to the Father? (3).

39   Our identification of these issues in our earlier Report has
led us to concentrate upon the following five issues:

priesthood and the representation of God in Christ

priesthood, headship and the exercise of authority

**priesthood, the unity of the church, and the authority of
the ordained ministry**

**Scripture, tradition, reason: how the sources of
Christian authority are used in this debate**

**decision making when there is division in the universal
Church.**

40   The House of Bishops has been encouraged by the agreement that
exists among us on many matters relating to these five issues. We
have explored those areas on which we remain divided within the
context of that larger agreement. We do, however, have to record
that there remain some crucial matters at the heart of the debate
on which there is no agreement amongst us. Moreover these
differences lead us to take different views about whether it is
right, appropriate, or opportune for the Church of England to
ordain women to the priesthood.

41   We offer the fruits of our discussion in the hope that, as the
legislation is debated in the synods of the Church of England,
that debate will be informed by theological judgement and that the
integrity of those who hold opinions at variance with their own
will be acknowledged and respected. The manner in which members
of the Church of England conduct this debate will say something

about what we believe about our life together in the communion of
the Holy Spirit. We believe the Holy Spirit will guide the Church
as it seeks to come to a mind on the ordination of women to the
priesthood.

Chapter 2

PRIESTHOOD AND THE REPRESENTATION OF GOD IN CHRIST

42   We have come to recognise that the issue of representation is
a crucial issue in the current debate. Who may appropriately
represent God in Christ? The God to be represented is the one we
apprehend as source of all things, the author of our salvation,
the origin of the Church. God is Creator, the Almighty; God is
also the one who empties himself and takes our flesh, the
suffering servant; and God is the giver of life. By faith we know
God as Trinity: three equal persons co-existing, co-inhering and
corresponding with one another in perfect unity. From the Son,
whose work is to do the will of the one who sent him, we perceive
that the equality and perfect mutuality of the Trinity also
entails order. Taught by Scripture and by Christ himself, we
address God as 'our Father'. In Jesus' language about God
'Father' is not only an image; it is primarily the name of God.
The language of Father and Son must not be relinquished. Scripture
also speaks of God's care for his people as maternal. But God is
not masculine, neither is God feminine. God is the source of
masculine and feminine and of all those characteristics which are
variously called masculine and feminine in different cultures.
The mystery of the Holy Trinity stretches our language to the
utmost limits: we can speak only in terms of allusion, of symbol,
of metaphor.

43   We are created men and women in the image of God. In baptism,
through faith, we are brought to share in the life of the Trinity
as members of the Body of Christ. There is a sense in which every
man and woman, created in God's image, represents God. But all

baptised persons have a special ministry by virtue of their
baptism into the death and resurrection of Christ to represent God
in Christ in the world. **We are all agreed that in this general
sense both men and women are representatives of God in Christ.
Further, we are all agreed that women, on occasions, and in
particular ways, represent the community of the Church.** Women
bring gifts and lead prayers in the worship of the Church, both at
the eucharist and at other services; on behalf of the congregation
women represent the people in local, national, international
councils. Those of us who are opposed to the ordination of women
do not deny the appropriateness of women representing God, or the
people of God, in these general ways. Genesis 1.27 affirms:

> God created man in his own image, in the image of God he
> created him; male and female he created them.

This makes clear that both women and men by virtue of their
humanity show forth something of the divine nature. This kind of
general representation contributes to our stumbling attempts to
give expression to our apprehensions of the nature and being of
God who is beyond the constraints of gender.

44   **The issue of representation and priesthood, however, goes
beyond this general understanding of being a representative
person. It concerns a particular way in which the ordained
priesthood is understood as representing Christ.**

45   **We are all agreed that there is a particular sense in which,
by virtue of ordination, a priest becomes a representative person.**
This act of ordination brings the ordinand into a particular
relationship with Christ and the Christian community. This
relationship, in that it is abiding and not episodic, is sometimes
described in terms of the 'character' of ordination (see <u>Canons of
the Church of England</u> C.1,2). This is a relationship of oversight
and responsibility within the people of God. It relates

especially to that which is fundamentally constitutive of the Church: the ministry of Word and Sacraments. There is a limited but proper sense in which the ordained person - especially the bishop but also the presbyter - has a commission in ordination to act in the name of Christ the Head of the Church. Article XXVI speaks of ministers as exercising the ministry of Word and Sacraments not in their own name but in Christ's. Thus those who are called to this ministry are ordained to speak and act not only in the name of the Christian community, but also in the name of Christ in relation to the community. This is the ministerial priesthood.

46   This ministry of Word and Sacraments finds a particular focus in the priest's liturgical role in the eucharist at which he presides over the proclamation of the Word, whether or not he himself preaches, as well as the celebration of the Lord's Supper. In the eucharistic prayer he leads the people and recites the words of Christ as the Church calls to mind the one sacrifice of Christ on the Cross, his death, resurrection and ascension, and looks forward to his coming in glory. Thus in the celebration of the eucharist the ministerial priest acts in the name of Christ the Head of the Church, both as the Lord who has offered himself for his people, and as the Lord who offers his people, in, with and through himself, to his Father.

47   **Accordingly we are all agreed that - as Article XXVI says - in the celebration of the Word and Sacraments ministers act in the name of Christ.** Although deacons share in the ministry of the Word, in the administration of baptism, and the solemnisation of matrimony, the presidency of the eucharist is reserved to bishops and presbyters who are particularly called to be ministers of Christ the Shepherd and Priest.

23

48   We differ in two crucial but interrelated matters as regards priesthood and representation:

> - first, what is implied in our common belief that a priest is called to represent Christ?
> - secondly, what are the implications of changes in sacramental symbolism?

(i) The Priest as a Representative of Christ

49   The priest is called to represent Christ. Some understand this as meaning that when the priest represents Christ he does this as his **representative,** not in any sense as a representation of Christ. Professor Geoffrey Lampe put it this way:

> The ambassador represents the Queen. He acts in her name; he speaks for her....but he is not a representation of the Queen. He does not impersonate her. He need not be a woman; nor when a queen succeeds a king do all the sovereign's representatives have to be replaced if they are men, by women (4).

Those of us who hold this view are not, therefore, swayed by arguments which depend upon a supposed need for the priest to resemble the Christ whom he represents.

50   Those of us in favour of the ordination of women to the presbyterate do not wish to discount the proper sense in which the priest speaks and acts in Christ's name nor to deny that the priesthood has a sacramental quality. With the Second Vatican Council, moreover, they would want to emphasise that the priest acts in the image of Christ the eternal High Priest throughout the entire eucharistic celebration. The priest is not therefore to be understood as enacting or imitating the role of the earthly Jesus at the Last Supper. The eucharist is a sacrament of the Church rather than a passion play. In the eucharistic prayer it is significant that the institution narrative refers to Jesus Christ in the third person, hos', 'qui', 'who'. The eucharistic prayer is always addressed through Jesus Christ to the Father.

51   Others of us, however, understand the belief that the priest represents Christ in a much stronger sense than this. There is, on this view, a particular sense in which the priest acts 'in persona Christi', as 'alter Christus'. This is most clearly seen in the eucharist when the priest says the Prayer of Consecration. This view is summed up in the Roman Catholic Declaration Inter Insigniores on the question of the admission of women to the ministerial priesthood (1976):

> The Church's constant teaching...declares that the bishop or the priest, in the exercise of his ministry, does not act in his own name in persona propria: he represents Christ, who acts through him: 'the priest truly acts in the place of Christ', as Saint Cyprian already wrote in the third century. It is this ability to represent Christ that Saint Paul considered as characteristic of his apostolic function (cf. 2 Cor 5:20; Gal. 4:14). The supreme expression of this representation is found in the altogether special form it assumes in the celebration of the Eucharist, which is the source and centre of the Church's unity, the sacrificial meal in which the People of God are associated in the sacrifice of Christ: the priest, who alone has the power to perform it, then acts not only through the effective power conferred on him by Christ, but in persona Christi, taking the role of Christ, to the point of being his very image, when he pronounces the words of consecration (5).

52   Behind this view there lies the understanding that the priest is a sacramental person, a sign whose effectiveness depends not only upon the authority conferred by ordination but also upon the human perceptibility of the sacramental sign. Sacraments, it is argued, are based upon natural signs, on symbols deeply embedded in the human psyche. As St Thomas Aquinas put it, 'Sacramental signs represent what they signify by natural resemblance'. This natural resemblance would be overthrown were a woman to preside at the eucharist.

53   **There are some of us who believe that as the priest represents Christ only men ought to be ordained.** It is not sufficient to

argue that the Christ represented is the glorious risen, ascended Christ and not the earthly Jesus. The risen Christ has a continuity with the crucified body of the earthly Jesus: the humanity taken into the Godhead in the resurrection and ascension is none other than the humanity assumed in the incarnation. **It is at this point in the argument about priesthood and the representation of God in Christ that the greatest difference of opinion among us has surfaced. As the priest represents Christ, and as there is continuity between the man Jesus of Nazareth and the risen, ascended Christ, some of us thus hold that only men may appropriately be ordained to the priesthood. Our disagreement turns upon our estimation of the significance of the maleness of Jesus.**

54 **Further, those of us who hold this view go on to argue that when in 'the fulness of time' the pre-existent Word became human in the form of a Jewish male there was a significance in the particularity of maleness; a significance which militates against the ordination of women to the priesthood.** Sexual differentiation, unlike Jewishness, belongs to a fundamental differentiation in the created order and has necessarily a significance over and above any significance that can be claimed for any other particularity. Moreover, the incarnation of God as a male was not a necessary consequence of the limitation of choice imposed by human nature in two kinds. Neither was it imposed by the particular cultural circumstances which in the first century A.D. would have limited the ministry of a woman. Rather, the incarnation of the Son of God as a male is consonant with the character of God as known through creation and revelation. The correspondence between the character of God perceived in God's self-revelation, and what is understood about the character of male humanity, is consonant with the incarnation of the Son of God as male. While it ought not be thought that there is any sexual

26

differentiation within the Godhead, the Word had to be incarnate as either a man or a woman. It is congruous with the nature of God as he relates to humanity that the Word should have become a man. Male humanity reflects God known through creation and revelation in a way that female humanity does not.

55 There are thus some of us who understand that God's relationship to the world is essentially 'male-like' and 'masculine'. Those of us who argue like this do not believe that God is a male but that God relates to creation, made by, for and in himself, in a 'male-like' and 'masculine' and not a 'female-like' and 'feminine' manner. In terms of our relationship to God we are essentially 'female-like' and feminine and he is 'male-like' and masculine. God always has the initiative and our duty is to respond. Because, psychologically and symbolically and, to an important extent, biologically, taking the initiative is male, it was therefore appropriate that the Word was incarnate as a male human being and not as a female human being. The particularity of maleness assumed in the incarnation and taken into the Godhead signifies divine initiative.

56 This view of the significance of maleness in the incarnation depends upon an understanding both of the nature of God and also upon a particular understanding of the basic differentiation between the sexes, a view which is held by some, though not by all, psychologists. The differentiation between the sexes is summed up by Dr Mary Rousseau thus:

> sexuality is not accidental but essential to our
> personal identity....God and the world, Spirit and
> matter, eternity and time and other pairs of opposites
> are not linked in dichotomous chaos, but are unified in
> a bipolar reciprocity that is orderly and good. The
> bipolarity of masculine and feminine, however, is not
> just one of reciprocity; it is rather the basic
> structure of reality, and as such, it is sacramental.
> Sexual roles are holy because they are ontological, not
> just functional. To be masculine is to worship as a

causal symbol of God's steadfast love for his creation,
and to be feminine is to worship as an image of
creation's acceptance of that love (6).

**From such an estimation of the nature of God and the nature of the
sexes, some of us believe that it is thus congruous for the
priest, the one who represents the divine initiative in Christ, to
be a man who is a symbol of that masculinity. It would thus be
incongruous to ordain a woman.**

57   Those of us who argue that the choice of a male person in the
incarnation is wholly consistent with the nature of God believe
that the incarnation in fact shows further how the two sexes are
related. It was male human nature that the Son of God united to
his divine nature but it was female human nature that was chosen
to be the bearer of the divine Son of God (cf para. 30). Thus the
incarnation from one point of view affirms male humanity above
female and from another point of view it exalts female human
nature. The economy of salvation witnessed
in the respective roles of Jesus and of Mary is of such
significance that it has necessarily to be reflected in the life
and ministry of the Church. When God took human nature, God chose
to express himself in that mode which in human life expresses the
divine giving, the divine initiative. God always takes the
initiative; this we see characteristically in, for instance, the
exodus and the resurrection as much as in the incarnation. Thus
God calls upon men to do that within the Church which reminds us
always that, whether we are worshipping or being blessed or being
absolved, it is God who gives, God who takes the initiative and
God to whom we must respond. It is the special vocation of Mary,
and therefore of all Christian women, to exercise the
complementary role of witnessing to total self-giving in love and
obedience. Women thus bear a particular task of witnessing to
self-giving, a self-giving which is in fact the response demanded

of all, men and women, priests and laity, to that divine initiative. The witnessing roles of men and women are therefore distinct, yet complementary. They each bear a message which carries a significance for all human beings.

58   The significance of male and female, masculine and feminine, seen in the man Jesus and the woman Mary, are parallel in other male/masculine, female/feminine images in Scripture. So God is 'Our Father' in relation to humanity and Christ is Head, Lord and Bridegroom, in relation to the Church. The image of Christ as Bridegroom describes the work of redemption in terms of the man - woman relationship. This is a theme worked out in some detail in Ephesians 5. Christ is Head of the Church and the Church, as the bride of Christ, is to be subject to him as a wife is to her husband. The relation between a man and his wife conveys a great truth about the Church. In his letter to the Archbishop of Canterbury, Cardinal Willebrands echoes this theme of the congruity between male/masculine and female/feminine images used in the biblical writing. He sees this as appropriately reflected in an all male priesthood:

> The picture of human redemption that is now before us in the Scriptures is of a God who is powerful to save and of a people who receive salvation as a free gift. Feminine imagery is used to reveal the place of the human family in God's plan of salvation. In the Old Testament, the people of Israel are depicted as the bride of Yahweh. In the New Testament St. Paul speaks of the Church as the bride of Christ. In its tradition, the Church has understood itself in terms of this feminine imagery and symbolism as the Body which received the Word of God, and which is fruitful in virtue of that which has been received. Mary, the Mother of God, is, in her response to the Word of God, a type of Church. Christ, on the other hand, is the Head of the Body, and it is through the Head that the whole Body is redeemed. It is precisely in this perspective that the representative role of the ministerial priesthood is to be understood.
>
> Christ took on human nature to accomplish the redemption of all humanity. But as Inter Insigniores says 'we can

never ignore the fact that Christ is a man'. His male
identity is an inherent feature of the economy of
salvation, revealed in the Scriptures and pondered in
the Church. The ordination only of men to the
priesthood has to be understood in terms of the intimate
relationship between Christ the redeemer and those who,
in a unique way, co-operate in Christ's redemptive work.
The priest represents Christ in His saving relationship
with His Body the Church. He does not primarily
represent the priesthood of the whole People of God.
However unworthy, the priest stands in persona Christi.
Christ's saving sacrifice is made present in the world
as a sacramental reality in and through the ministry of
priests. And the sacramental ordination of men takes on
force and significance precisely within this context of
the Church's experience of its own identity, of the
power and significance of the person of Jesus Christ,
and of the symbolic and iconic role of those who
represent him in the Eucharist. (cf Appendix)

59   In the argument as we have outlined it above, and as that
argument appears in the letter of Cardinal Willebrands, the
particularity of maleness in the incarnation is not contingent or
peripheral: it is consistent with the nature of God. God's way of
being with us as a human is wholly consistent with God's way of
being God. Maleness, unlike Jewishness, is thus a fundamental of
Jesus' identity and points beyond human differentiation to the
very character of God. It is humanity, with the integral quality
of maleness, and with all the significance that maleness carries,
which was taken up into the Godhead at the resurrection and
ascension of Jesus Christ. All of this leads some of us to the
conclusion that if a priest is to be a 'representation', an 'image
of Christ', it is supremely appropriate that the ordained priest
should be male and not female. **Some of us who cannot accept the
ordination of women as priests believe that the pattern of
creation itself is reflected in God's choice to be incarnate as a
male. And, moreover, that that choice would be obscured, even
denied, if a woman were the sacramental sign of divine initiative:
thus the essential dependence of humanity upon God would be
brought into question. Further, they believe that a male human**

being can be as representative of all humanity as a male. Jesus
Christ embraces and represents the whole of humanity. A major
change in the Church's ministry is not therefore justified merely
on the grounds that it would witness to that fact. If such witness
be necessary they would ask why divine providence would have left
us without it for nearly two thousand years.

60   There are others of us who find the argument set out above
impossible to accept as an argument against the ordination of
women. Because they believe that both men and women are redeemed
by Jesus Christ, they therefore hold that to ordain both men and
women to the priesthood would witness to the inclusiveness of that
redemption. It is not the particularity of the maleness of Jesus,
either in the incarnation or in the form of humanity taken into
the Godhead at the ascension which is of determinative
significance, but rather humanity itself. In the prologue of St
John's Gospel and in the Nicene Creed the emphasis in the
incarnation is upon the Word becoming human, rather than upon the
Word becoming a male person. Indeed, if it is not inclusive
humanity that is taken up into the Godhead then what implication
does that have for the salvation of half of the human race, for
'what he did not assume, he did not heal' (7)?

61   To concentrate too exclusively on the significance of the
maleness of Jesus in the incarnation, whether used to argue for or
against the ordination of women, is to lose something of the
primary emphasis of the biblical and the patristic writing upon
the humanity of Jesus. The early writers show no interest in the
maleness of Jesus as such, but point to the limitations, weakness
and suffering which were accepted by the Word - something common
to all humanity, male and female. Professor R. Norris has
demonstrated this in the writings of Justin Martyr.

      For Justin Martyr...the point of the incarnation is
      conveyed by mention of the divine Word's birth and

31

crucifixion, as well as his death and resurrection - all
of which is summed up in the statement that he 'became
man' (anthropos)...this language of Justin's is
calculated to draw attention to the same truth as does
that of the New Testament. What is important
christologically about the humanity of Jesus is not its
Jewishness, its maleness, or any other such
characteristic, but simply the fact that he was 'like
his brethren in every respect'...In the age of the great
christological controversies, the terms anthropos and
anthropotes became the normative equivalents of the
Johannine 'flesh'. This usage is canonized in the
Nicene Symbol where the verb enanthropein is used in
effect to explain the meaning of 'became flesh'. The
growing prevalence of this usage gradually (and not
indeliberately) excluded the employment of 'body' as the
equivalent of 'flesh'; for the latter custom appeared to
encourage, if not to require, an Apollinaristic
truncation of Jesus' humanity. The Fathers became sure
that in speaking of the incarnation one must emphasise
both the wholeness and (therefore) the inclusiveness of
Jesus' humanity. It was strictly necessary, for the
sake of mankind's salvation, that Jesus be integrally
the same sort of being as those whom he saves. This is
the ultimate implication of Gregory Nazianzen's well
known assertion against Apollinarius: What is not
assumed is not healed (8).

The early Fathers had to resist constant attempts to narrow the
salvation won by Christ, lest it ceased to be truly inclusive of
the whole human race throughout the ages and the world. They were
not interested in maleness, and therefore cannot help us in
determining what, if any, is the soteriological significance of
the fact that Jesus was born as a man and not as a woman, nor
whether this has any bearing on the nature of the ordained
priesthood.

62   The argument set out in paras 51 - 58 depends upon two further
premises. The first concerns a particular understanding about the
nature of God: the second concerns a particular understanding of
the basic differentiation between the sexes. There are those of
us who would wish to challenge both of these premises.

63   First, no-one can deny that the God of the Old Testament and
the God of the New Testament is a God who takes the initiative in
creation and redemption. But to describe this initiative as
'male-like' or 'masculine' distorts the total picture of God
revealed to us in the Bible. The God who humbles himself in
obedience on the Cross receiving insults, humiliation and torture,
achieving thereby the redemption of the world, is acting in a way
which cannot be described adequately as 'masculine' or 'feminine'.

64   The recent report of the Doctrine Commission, We Believe in
God had this to say about a tendency in the past to emphasise the
'masculine characteristics' in God:

> In cultures in which power, authority and education are
> typically in the hands of men it is inevitable that God
> should be pictured with predominantly masculine
> characteristics. Yet here again the Bible offers a
> wider range of attributes. God is occasionally
> described in terms of tenderness and longsuffering
> vigilance usually thought more appropriate to motherhood
> than fatherhood. Jesus, too, uses imagery of himself
> (that of a hen gathering her chicks) which points in the
> same direction. Our own generation, with its concern
> for the equality and complementarity of the sexes,
> invites fresh attention to this aspect of the biblical
> tradition, so that the richness of Scripture's
> perception of God may enlarge our imagining to press
> beyond our own restricted models and categories of
> gender towards the ultimate mystery of God (9).

God is neither male nor female, and those qualities we call
'masculine' and 'feminine', which we all, men and women, share in
varying admixture, are encompassed and transcended in the
wholeness of divine life and love. Further, the re-emphasis in
some recent theology on the view of the Trinity as relational, on
what is called 'the social Trinity' in which each person of the
Trinity is perfectly open to the other and interdependent in a
relationship of mutual giving and receiving, provides a different
emphasis in understanding the nature of God. It points to a

complementarity in the nature of God rather than a single emphasis upon the initiating and so called 'male-like' and 'masculine' character of God.

65   Secondly, the earlier argument of paras 51-58 depended also upon an understanding of the basic nature of men and women which some of us find hard to accept. It depends upon an understanding of sexual difference which does not reflect the views of all psychologists. Some psychologists hold that while there are obvious biological differences between the sexes, there is no justification within psychology for maintaining that men and women are fundamentally and inherently different. Neither is there any justification for assuming that the so called 'masculine' characteristics belong to men only and that the so called 'feminine' characteristics belong to women only. Every man and every woman share in a varying admixture those qualities we have come to designate as masculine and feminine. 'The more we combine in ourselves those attitudes and attributes traditionally seen as feminine and as masculine, the more adjusted and mature a person we are' (10). Such a psychological estimate would suggest that to limit so called 'masculine' characteristics to men, and so called 'feminine' characteristics to women, is to destroy our way of being human and to have a detrimental effect upon our relationships. To categorise initiative taking as masculine and male, and receptivity as feminine and female, and to assign them severally to men and to women, is to fall into a trap of destructive stereotyping. In doing this, human growth and potential is limited. Furthermore, it does not do justice to the way in which many men and women experience relationships of mutual giving and receiving, receiving and giving.

66   **Some of us believe that if women are ordained to the priesthood, the ordained ministry would be a more complete**

34

representation of God in Christ than an all male priesthood: it would emphasise the richness of humanity taken by the Word in the incarnation: it would make clear the inclusive quality of the risen and glorified humanity that is eternally a part of the Godhead and witness to a belief that God embraces and transcends male and female, masculine and feminine. To argue that to ordain a woman to the priesthood would obscure the sacramental sign of divine initiative is therefore seen by some of us as to misunderstand both the nature of God and the nature of women and men, created in God's image, and of their relationship the one to another. Instead of obscuring something true in the nature of God, the ordination of women to the priesthood would bring a complementarity and wholeness to the ministry and thus reflect a wholeness that belongs to the nature of God as God has been revealed to us.

67 There is then a fundamental disagreement amongst us on the question of the significance of the maleness of Jesus. For some of us the fact that Jesus was male is determinative for the question of the ordination of women to the priesthood: it precludes women's ordination. Maleness assumed by God in the incarnation corresponds to something in the nature of God as he relates to us in a way that femaleness does not. Maleness reflects the fact that the initiative is always with God in a way that femaleness does not. The way God chose to be human is consonant with the basic nature of humanity as created by God. It therefore follows that only men can represent God in Christ as priests. Others of us are not, however, convinced by this argument. The fact that God became human is the central message of the incarnation. Moreover, they cannot accept the emphasis placed upon the powerful initiating character of God identified as 'male-like' and masculine without at the same time holding in balance the complementary receiving character of God's nature.

They are unhappy about a too marked differentiation between sexual characteristics which forms a part of the argument.

(ii) The Significance of Sacramental Symbols

68 The argument about priesthood and representation is related to the significance of sacramental symbols in the life of the Church. The sacraments of the Church are the covenanted means by which God bridges the gap between himself and his people and makes possible here and now an encounter with the living, ascended Christ. In the sacraments Christ's continuing saving action is visible on earth and freely available. By means of sacraments the communion of Christians with God and with one another in Christ is established, maintained and strengthened. Sacraments are not 'things' but encounters of women and men with the risen and glorified Christ: they are visible and tangible signs of the saving, heavenly action of Christ. While the presence and gift of God does not depend upon the faith of those who receive the sacrament, faith is needed to discern the sacramental gift of God. Our response to God's gift of himself in sacramental signs is a vital part of the efficacy of the sacramental life of the Church as it lives within the New Covenant.

(a) Matter and form

69 Some people argue that to ordain a woman would in fact be to change or modify the 'matter' of the sacrament of Holy Order. In the course of history there have been some modifications to the 'matter' of the sacrament of the eucharist: leavened and unleavened bread, and, in some traditions, unfermented grape juice have been used. In confirmation there has been an oscillation between the laying on of hands and anointing as the 'matter' of confirmation. In ordination, however, whilst theologians have argued about what constitutes the form and the matter (in respect

36

of the prayer of ordination, its form and content; and the action which accompanies the prayer, the laying on of hands and/or the porrectio instrumentorum) at no time has it in fact been claimed that a male person constitutes valid 'matter'. It is, therefore, difficult to sustain an argument against ordaining women simply by asserting that to so ordain a woman would be to change the 'matter' of the sacrament.

(b) Natural resemblance

70   In baptism the washing with water is accompanied by the baptismal prayer: in the eucharist the taking of bread and wine is accompanied by the Eucharistic Prayer which has traditionally included the Words of Institution: in ordination the laying on of hands is accompanied by the liturgical prayer.   In the two dominical sacraments, baptism and eucharist, there is a natural congruity between the celebration of the sacrament and what is signified: between water and the act of washing, and between bread and wine and the act of eating and drinking. Similarly, it is argued, there is a natural congruity between the person being ordained and the work and office for which he is being thus ordained, namely the task of representing Jesus Christ in the ministry entrusted to the apostles. Underlying such an assertion is the view that the sacramental system is in fact based upon natural signs and symbols. As noted in paragraph 51, St Thomas Aquinas writes: 'Sacramental signs represent what they signify by natural resemblance', and this naturalness of resemblance goes for persons as well as for things. At the celebration of the eucharist Christ is recognised in the proclamation of the Word and the celebrating of the sacrament as well as in the presence of those gathered for worship. **And some of us believe that the need for the naturalness of resemblance between Christ and the celebrant, symbolised in a male rather than a female person, continues to be**

a proper requirement. For those of us who hold this view to
ordain a woman would obscure the clarity of the sacramental sign,
thereby introducing a major shift in the hitherto unbroken
tradition of the church. There are others of us, however, who
believe that such a step ought to be made. They regard it rather
as an enriching of the sacramental sign. Such a step would
indicate the inclusiveness of the whole of humanity in the person
of the celebrant.

(c) Doubt about the efficacy of the sacrament

71   Whatever view we take on the ordination of women we all
recognise that there exists a proper concern about the 'subject'
of the sacramental action in ordination. The ordained priest is
integrally related to the sacramental sign of both ordination and
the eucharist. There are those of us who are concerned that to
change the sex of the person ordained, or to change the sex of the
celebrant of the eucharist, would inevitably raise fears about the
efficacy of the sacrament and prevent people from approaching God
with confidence and without presumption. And, although the
sacramental gift is not itself dependent upon the faith response
of the individual, nevertheless faith is necessary to discern
God's gift. The fears of those who feel that the reliability of
the sacrament itself would be endangered by a change in the sex of
the ordained person ought not to be treated lightly, for such a
change would endanger their response of faith. Those of us for
whom this is a serious argument against the ordination of women
agree that there are areas in matters of faith where action may be
taken, even before the mind of the Church is clear and in spite of
remaining areas of doubt and perplexity. Nevertheless, they
believe that this cannot be the case where doubt concerns the
efficacy of a sacrament. **They hold that in all cases where doubt
concerns the efficacy of a sacrament the 'safer' course must be**

followed. It is a basic moral principle that doubt must not be created about the ministry which is the sacramental means of grace instituted by Christ. (Article XXVI is designed to remove doubt in the case of evil ministers).

72   Many of us, however, would welcome, or at least find acceptable, the ordination of women. **They do not believe such a step would endanger the efficacy of the sacraments.** However they recognise the need for sensitivity in relation to those whose faith in the efficacy of the sacraments would be shaken were a woman to be ordained to the priesthood and to preside at the eucharist. Nevertheless, they believe that it is an action to be taken confidently if, or when, the Church of England determines, through synodical processes, to proceed. The risk involved has to be seen in the light of the richer significance and more credible sign of the kingdom to which an inclusive ordained ministry would bear witness. Those of us who hold this believe that the experience of women priests will in time convince those with doubt that the efficacy of the sacrament is not impaired. Further, the faith of the community in which the majority affirm the ordination of women will sustain the doubt of the individual. However, those of us who believe the Church right to proceed to ordain women take seriously the need to care pastorally for those who strongly disagree with such action.

(d) Apostolic continuity

73   There is a further related matter. Both bishops and priests are important signs to the Christian community of the apostolic continuity of the Church and a sign of its unity. Although the apostolic continuity of the Church is related to the Church's fidelity to the teaching and mission of the apostles, the ministry is not a guarantee of apostolic succession; nevertheless the

ministry (in particular, the episcopal ministry) is a sign of apostolic succession. It serves, symbolises and guards the continuity of the apostolic faith and communion. It therefore needs to be considered whether a change in the sign of apostolicity would endanger, or call in question, the fidelity of the Church to the apostolic faith itself. Jesus was a man, the apostles were male, and the ordained ministry for nearly two thousand years has been almost exclusively male. Would the ordination of women to the episcopate and presbyterate put in question the fidelity of the Church to its call to apostolicity? Would the sign of apostolicity cease to be an 'effective sign' if those ordained were to include both men and women?

74   Some of us believe that the apostolicity of the Church would not be called into question by the ordination of women. Others of us believe that there is a danger. Further, this danger is increased if action were to be taken by only one part of the universal Church.

(iii) Summary

75   In reflecting upon the issue of representation and priesthood we have found that there is much upon which we all agree. The understanding of priesthood and the call to the priest to act in a particular way in the name of Christ, that is to represent Christ, are not issues that divide us: neither is our understanding of sacramentality and the importance of sacramental signs. Rather, our fundamental disagreement lies in the different weight we place upon the significance of the maleness of Jesus in the incarnation and the relation of that maleness both to the nature of God and also to the nature of men and women created in God's image. We believe this question lies at the heart of the Church's current debate. We are also divided on the admissibility of extending the

priesthood to include women while there are those who would hold such action to be a threat to the efficacy of the sacraments. We are further divided on the question of the gravity of one part of the universal Church unilaterally changing the 'sign' of apostolicity in so obvious a manner.

Chapter 3

PRIESTHOOD, HEADSHIP AND THE EXERCISE OF AUTHORITY

76   In the previous chapter we discussed the issue of the role of
the priest in representing God in Christ and the particular
bearing that this has on the question of the ordination of women
to the priesthood. Closely related to that theme is the issue of
priesthood, headship and the exercise of authority in the Church.
**We are all agreed that one aspect of ordination is to set a person
apart for leadership, oversight and responsibility within the
community of the Church. We are also agreed that a bishop or a
presbyter has a commission to 'act in the name of Christ', of the
Christ who is Head of the Church: the bishop and also the
presbyter exercise a role of 'headship' in relation to the
community.** Leadership which is called to imitate Christ as Head of
the Church, is to be exercised with those qualities of servanthood
which we see in the ministry of Jesus in the New Testament. As
Head of the Church he is the one who came 'not to be served but to
serve and to give his life a ransom for many'. The diaconal
quality of ministry is not confined to the order of deacons but is
to permeate all ministry in Christ's name including the ministry
of oversight.

77   **There are some among us who believe that while women are
legitimately ordained within the threefold order as deacons they
may not be ordained as bishops or as priests. It is inappropriate
for women to be ordained to an order whose function is to exercise
authority and leadership over the community, an order moreover
called to represent the ministry of Christ, the Head of the
Church.** The reason for this lies in Scripture: in particular in
what the Bible says about the significance of female and male in

42

the created order, and the view put forward in certain texts that man is 'head of woman', as Christ is 'Head of the Church'. This biblical understanding of men and women has particular relevance for the ordination of women as bishops, but also for the ordination of women as priests, for the bishop shares his exercise of oversight and leadership with his presbyters.

78 The issue of priesthood, headship and the exercise of authority raises the question of the significance of male and female in the created order and is thus integrally bound up with the issue explored in the preceding chapter. In that chapter we recognised that there are those among us who believe that it is inappropriate for a woman to be ordained to a priesthood which represents the priesthood of Christ. This is because of an understanding of the fundamental difference between the sexes. Those of us who hold this view base our estimate of sexual differentiation not only upon observations of biology, psychology and sociology but also upon an understanding of the witness of the Old and New Testaments and the Church's continuing tradition. Thus the biblical view of the relationship of the sexes has to be grappled with and brought to bear on the debate.

(i) The Use of Scripture

79 When we come to search the Scriptures for guidance we come as those who seek to be open to what the Spirit is saying to us through their authoritative and normative witness. But we recognise that we each bring many assumptions with us. We are all influenced in our interpretation of Scripture by the particular group in the Christian community in which we have been nurtured: catholic or evangelical, conservative or liberal. And our individual experience of the society around us and our personal relationships all contribute to the way in which we interpret the

43

Bible. Further, we acknowledge that, as bishops, we presently exercise authority in the Church as part of an all male college of bishops which, even if unconsciously, may have an effect upon the way we think about the particular issue of the exercise of authority in the Church. Each one of us brings to the task of biblical interpretation a conditioned mind: there is no such thing as 'neutrality' in our approach to the Scriptures. Nevertheless, we have an obligation to go back again and again to the Scriptures for guidance.

80   When we turn to the Bible for guidance we have to wrestle with particular passages, asking why the passage was included in the Canon, what relevance each passage has in its canonical context, and also what was the particular situation for which it was written or spoken. The biblical passages which bear upon an understanding of the nature of men and women come from a long period of time covering almost two thousand years. The roles and relationships of women and men in the time of the Old Testament patriarchs developed in the context of the nomadic way of life of tribal peoples: this was a very different context from the view of first century Palestine, influenced as it was by Graeco-Roman culture. Even those passages which are Pauline reflect very different local situations and address different social problems. Moreover, none of the passages sets out to be a comprehensive treatise on the nature of women and men and their relationships: what we learn we learn indirectly as the writers face particular theological issues or practical problems. We need to ask, what situation does the passage address and what truth was it safeguarding in its own day? Only when we have understood what it was saying in its own context can we move to ask what the message is for us in the twentieth century and how the truth intended by the passage can be most convincingly conveyed today. This process is commonly referred to as 'hermeneutics'. Hermeneutics is the

exploration of how the message travels from one time and culture
to another. It involves an attempt to perceive how a text was
understood and appropriated in its original context; what
significance it has in its canonical position, how it relates to
the overall message of Scripture; how the continuing Christian
community has reflected upon it and interpreted it through
history, and how it now applies in our own time. For example,
what was it that Paul believed which made him issue directives
about the Corinthian women in Christian worship? The interpreter
has to try to discern, under the guidance of the Holy Spirit, what
theological conviction made this an appropriate injunction in the
circumstances and how that theological conviction might best be
upheld in the cultural context in which we proclaim the Christian
Gospel today. In relation to our subject it is clear that women's
position in society today is very different from that in apostolic
times or in the period in which the Genesis texts were written
down.

81   The same 'hermeneutical' process has also to be applied to
the tradition of the Church. We need to ask in each given
situation what theological conviction made this appropriate in the
circumstances? There is a hermeneutical question to be asked of
the Scriptures and also of the continuing tradition. Only after
we have engaged in this process can the authority of Scripture and
tradition inform statements on faith and order for our own church
in our generation. This is not a simple process; nevertheless an
attempt must be made by those seeking guidance from Scripture and
tradition to bridge the distance between the world of the writers
of the past and that of our own day.

82   We all agree that isolated biblical texts read out of context
cannot finally settle the matter of the ordination of women to the
priesthood. There are, however, a number of biblical texts which

45

have a special relevance for this debate. We have struggled together to understand these texts but have reached a common mind neither on their interpretation in their own context, nor on their relation to the overall message of the Scriptures; nor on their significance for our contemporary debate.

(ii) Headship and Subordination

83   Before examining some of the biblical texts we set out some thoughts on a question relating to our understanding of the relationship of men to women. In interpreting the biblical texts we found ourselves time and time again referring to the concepts of male headship and the subordination of women to men. It was, however, unclear what we each understood about the view of the biblical writers on headship or subordination; nor was it immediately obvious what any one of us understood by the terms.

84   Headship is not a concept that is either familiar or congenial to much contemporary understanding of the relationship between men and women. Everyday use of 'head' in a metaphorical sense carries implications of status and in some instances of an arbitrary exercise of power. These have no place in Christian relationships, let alone in relationships between men and women in Christ. Furthermore we all agree that a key element in our perception of the nature of Christian ministry as we follow the example and leadership of Christ is that such ministry is the self-denying ministry of the servant. Nevertheless some of us wish to affirm that, particularly within a Christian community, there is a God-given role and function of an enabling authority which properly belongs to men in their relationship with women, for the purpose of a harmonious ordering of the community in Christ. This is what they understand by the headship of men over women. The majority of us however do not find such a concept

46

helpful or part of God's intention for a redeemed creation or for the redeemed community. Nor do they believe that it is the intention of the New Testament writers to convey such an understanding.

85   The notion of subordination is closely related to the interpretation of headship and the understanding of the exercise of authority and leadership. We came to recognise that the word 'subordination' is used in very different ways: sometimes it is used in a positive sense, though more often in a negative sense. None of us supports a view of the subordination of women to men which implies an essential inequality of nature between men and women, or an inherent male right to domination in relationships in general, or in marriage in particular. Domination and subordination with this character is a product of the Fall, a consequence of the way in which sin distorts human patterns of relationship. There are those of us who prefer not to use the term subordination at all. They cannot find any sense in which it usefully or accurately describes God's intentions for the relationship between men and women, either in general or in the marriage relationship in particular. Others of us recognise a 'proper' subordination which is part of God's intended order in creation; a subordination which makes for true partnership and complementarity. Subordination of women to men is a part of an ordered relationship in which man is head of woman and is the one who is entrusted with authority and leadership. For those of us who hold this view this has particular relevance within the marriage relationship and within the ordering of the Christian community. This subordination of women to men does not rule out a proper mutual submission in love of men to women and women to men.

86   A consideration closely related to our understanding of the relationship between the sexes is whether, and in what ways, the

relationship between women and men is intended to mirror the relationships within the Trinity. There is a 'subordination' in the ordered relationship between the persons of the Trinity which does not imply an inferiority of essence. The Son is the begotten and the Sent, and is freely obedient to the will of the Father: and, as Second Adam, the head of a new humanity, Christ is to hand over the Kingdom to the Father. For some of us this understanding of 'proper subordination' in the Trinity holds a key to the understanding of the relationship between men and women. Within the marriage relationship and in the Church women are 'properly subordinate' to men, men are to exercise headship. Others of us, however, are convinced that the mutuality between the three persons of the Holy Trinity, the giving and receiving - receiving and giving love of the three persons, is the primary model for all human relationships. Those of us who hold this latter view do not believe that, on account of the sex of a person, authority and headship are to be assigned to men and not to women. Of course for the good ordering of society and of the Church, authority, leadership and headship have to be exercised. But some of us can see no theological reason why they have necessarily to be exercised by men over women. Moreover, within the marriage bond, women are not subordinate to men. Rather, the ordered relationship between husband and wife is based upon mutual submission in love which involves a shared authority, leadership and headship within the family.

87   We hope that these remarks on subordination, headship and authority will clarify some of the arguments in the exegesis of biblical passages that follows. It is not possible to give a detailed exegesis of each of the relevant passages. Nevertheless, we have tried to indicate why these passages are crucial in the debate and lead some of us to take our particular stand on the ordination of women.

(iii) Biblical Texts

Genesis 1 - 3

88   Genesis 1 - 3 is made up of at least two major sources and
contains two accounts of creation.   While it is interesting to see
the different perspectives and emphases of the accounts we cannot
ignore the fact of their present canonical form and relationship.
They have come down to us as an integrated whole. While they are
distinguishable and in a sense distinctive voices, the canonical
presentation of a harmonised story of the creation and the Fall
has also given an overall and particular stamp to the story: the
second, but in time earlier account of creation in Genesis
2.5-3.24 is read in the context of the account in Genesis 1, the
later account.

Genesis 1

89   In Genesis 1 the creation of man and woman comes as the
culmination of God's creative activity on the sixth day of
creation. We read:

> God created man in his own image, in the image of God he
> created him; male and female he created them. God
> blessed them and said, 'Be fruitful and increase, fill
> the earth and subdue it, rule over the fish in the sea,
> the birds of the heaven, and every living thing that
> moves upon the earth' (Genesis 1.27 and 28 NEB).

In this account of creation humanity is created male and female.
One sex is not elevated above the other nor distinguished from the
other apart from the descriptive terms male and female. Both are
placed over all other forms of life. Sexuality is a fundamental
part of God's good creation. Both man and woman are created in
the image and likeness of God. There have always been differing

49

interpretations of what is meant by 'the image of God' in Genesis
1 since any physical representation of God is ruled out. Most
interpretations have stressed that the image of God is represented
in every individual human being. For some that image is the
capacity of man and woman to 'be fruitful' and 'to have dominion',
both God-like activities as witnessed in God's creation of the
world. For others the image in both men and women is their
capacity as relational beings: as God relates to each one of us,
so each may relate to him. For yet others the image has been
understood as each individual's capacity to create or to make
moral judgements. The image has also been taken to refer to
original righteousness. A second group of interpretations takes
the image as referring not so much to the image in individual
human beings but to the image shown forth by men and women in
relationship. So Karl Barth, for example, understands the image
as lying in the relationship between man and woman, particularly
as that is expressed in the closest of human relationships, the
marriage bond. The relationship between a man and a woman
corresponds to the fact that God exists in relationship. In such
interpretations there has been a tendency in some writers to
emphasise the difference between the man and the woman. So St
Augustine pondering on the image of God in man and woman wrote
that:

> The woman together with her own husband is the image of
> God, so that the substance may be one image but when she
> is referred to separately in her capacity of helpmeet,
> which regards the woman herself alone, then she is not
> the image of God; but as regards the man alone, he is the
> image of God as fully and completely as when the woman
> too is joined with him (11).

Although none of us would want to follow such an interpretation we
acknowledge the negative effect that this has had upon many,
particularly upon women, and upon the outworking of roles in the
life of the Church and of society in the past.

90   Some of us believe that the most obvious interpretation of
Genesis 1.27 is that the image refers to the capacity of women and
men 'to be fruitful' and 'to have dominion'. Others of us hold
that the significance of the image lies in the fact that being
made in the image of God conveys the possibility of human
relationship with God. None of us can see in this passage on its
own any allusion to a basic differentiation between male and
female: it is the similarity of male and female that is
emphasised. However, there are those of us whose understanding of
the passage is determined by their reading of Genesis 2 and 3.

Genesis 2.5 - 3.24

91   The differences between the later account of creation in
chapter 1 and the earlier account in chapter 2 partly arise from
the different scope of each narrative. In Genesis 1 the creation
of humanity comes at the end of the creative process: humanity is
the apex of creation. In Genesis 2 man is created first, and
around him the animal kingdom and the natural world, then woman.
Adam is created first and then woman from a rib taken from the
side of Adam. That the story points beautifully to the closest of
human relationships between the sexes cannot be doubted. But
there are many puzzling questions.

WHAT IS THE SIGNIFICANCE OF ADAM BEING CREATED FIRST? The fact
that Adam was created first has certainly been taken by some as
proof of the primacy, in the sense of superiority, of man over
woman. None of us would endorse such a view. There are some of us
who believe that the fact that Adam was created first does imply a
priority for man which carries an implicit authority, an authority
which is to be manifested in the relationship of men to women.
The subordination of woman to man is part of the created order.
The priority of Adam in the creating activity of God has a

significance which has been picked up and developed in the writings of the New Testament. Others of us do not find that theme in the passage. It is at least possible that the intention of the author was to suggest that God created an 'earth creature' first, neither a male nor a female. Only after a rib was taken and enfleshed, forming a woman, did sexual distinction result, only then did male and female come to be at the same time. Such a view does away with there being a temporal priority in the creation of man before woman. Even if such an interpretation is not acceptable, and certainly there are no extant myths from the Ancient Near East to parallel such an interpretation, some of us find it impossible to argue that temporal priority carries with it subordination in any sense of that word. Form and order is a part of creation but temporal priority does not seem to suggest more than that. Indeed, it could be argued that as woman was created last, far from being secondary and subordinate, woman was rather the crown and apex of creation.

WHAT IMPLICATION IS THERE IN THE FACT THAT WOMAN IS CREATED FROM ADAM'S RIB? It has sometimes been argued, though none of us would accept such an argument, that women are inferior to men, created as woman was from such a small insignificant part of Adam's body. For all of us the significance of the story of the rib is to illustrate the relatedness of woman to man as distinct from all the rest of creation: woman and man are of the same nature. However, for some of us, there is also a sign in this passage of a subordination of woman to man. The passage talks of the woman created _for_ man. This significance is further borne out in the New Testament when Paul asserts woman was created _for_ man.

IS THERE ANY SIGNIFICANCE TO BE DRAWN FROM THE FACT THAT THE WOMAN IS BROUGHT TO THE MAN AND NAMED BY HIM? For some of us both the bringing of the woman to the man and the naming of her by the man

imply male authority and man as initiator of the household.
Others of us do not see such an authority implied in the story.
When Adam calls to the woman issha (the Hebrew word for woman) is
he really giving her a name? He does not use her name Eve, but
rather the generic word 'woman'. It is only later in the story of
the Fall that the woman is named Eve: that is precisely the point
at which authority is assumed by the man over the woman. It is
therefore by no means clear to some of us that the fact that woman
is called issha by Adam ought to be used to suggest male
authority.

**WHAT IS THE IMPLICATION OF THE DESIGNATION OF THE WOMAN AS
'HELPER'?** This has undoubtedly been interpreted by some in the
past as referring to the relation of an inferior to a superior.
Again none of us would see this implied here. We are all
impressed by the fact that the same Hebrew word ezer is applied no
less than fifteen times to Yahweh as Israel's helper. 'Helper',
far from being used of an inferior to a superior is used of a
superior to an inferior. Some of us, therefore, cannot see any
'qualitative' difference between the sexes implied in the word.
Others of us believe that is primary purpose is to point to a
supportive relationship: women were created to support men.

92   Each of these arguments is finely balanced. We are not all of
one mind on their implications. There are those of us who believe
that the Genesis 2 account of creation, no less than the Genesis 1
account, is concerned with the equal status of women and men and
intended above all to underline the fact that men and women share
the same nature and are made for unity and communion. The
narrative ought not to be interpreted as upholding any
subservience of women to men in the created order, and certainly
not inferiority. Subservience and domination come in with the
story of the Fall in Genesis 3: woman becomes subservient, man

53

domineering, and the original intention of the creator is damaged and distorted. **Some of us cannot find here any_statement about the authority of man over woman such as would preclude women's ordination. The texts ought not to be used to preclude the ordination of women either to priesthood or to the episcopate.**

93 Others of us do believe that the creation narratives testify to a subordination of women and men in the created order itself. However, this subordination ought not to be equated with the destructive subordination which was the result of the Fall. It certainly cannot be equated with the 'inherent inferiority' proclaimed by some patristic and mediaeval theologians. It was this tradition of rightful subordination that Paul knew and continued to uphold in his ministry. This forms the background to his teaching. Further, that proper subordination reflects the subordination of the Son to the Father (c.f. para. 86). In addition the narratives point to an authority of man over woman. Male authority is to be understood primarily in terms of authority for enabling. In exercising this authority men are characteristically men, and in being subject to that authority women are characteristically women. Thus there is built into the order of creation a difference of function which belongs to each sex. **For some of us there is a divine ordinance in creation which precludes women being in positions of headship/leadership in the Christian community: it is therefore inappropriate, and indeed, against nature, for a woman to be in a ministry which is called to represent Christ the Head of the Church.**

94 **Others of us are less sure about the precise interpretation of the Genesis texts and believe, in the light of this uncertainty, no particular doctrine can be found from them.** Having examined the arguments on both sides it is impossible to be certain, beyond any doubt, about the precise meaning of the texts.

54

95   When we turn to the New Testament writers, understanding of the relationship between the sexes we find them influenced by their reading of the Old Testament Scriptures. Paul in particular draws upon the early narrative of Genesis to illustrate his teaching about ordered relationships in the Christian communities to which he writes and about the relationship of men and women in the marriage bond. He understood the Old Testament in the context of his own day. This can be seen particularly in his use of the story of Adam and Eve's fall from grace. Each situation to which the Apostle writes is different: sometimes he is addressing the relationship of men and women within marriage, sometimes the ordering of the Christian community and the Church's ministry. All of this needs to be taken into account as we assess the underlying belief about the relationships of the sexes expressed in any one particular passage.

(1) 1 Corinthians 11.2-16

96   In 1 Corinthians 11 Paul talks of man as 'head' (kephale) of woman as Christ is 'Head of the Church': a woman must acknowledge this by wearing a veil when she prays and prophesies. In the course of his argument Paul, echoing Genesis, writes:

> A man has no need to cover his head, because man is the image of God, and the mirror of his glory, whereas woman reflects the glory of man. For man did not originally spring from woman, but woman was made out of man; and man was not created for woman's sake, but woman for the sake of man; and therefore it is woman's duty to have a sign of authority* on her head, out of regard for the angels. And yet, in Christ's fellowship woman is as essential to man as man to woman. If woman was made out of man, it is through woman that man now comes to be; and God is the source of all (1 Cor. 11.7-12, NEB). *veil RSV.

There are complex questions raised by the vocabulary of the passage and the swift movements in Paul's thoughts. Nevertheless,

there are some of us who believe that the plain sense of the text
is that, for Paul, in the created order women are 'subordinate' to
men: that is the meaning of 'man is head (kephale) of woman'.
They recognise kephale has other meanings. Nevertheless when the
word is used metaphorically by Paul here, as in some other New
Testament contexts, the idea of headship is the primary meaning.
(Even if the word is understood as meaning 'source' they still
believe that the notion of authority is inherent in the word cf
para. 77). This is further supported by Paul's references back to
the text of Genesis 2. Paul's use of the Genesis text suggests
that he himself understood the Old Testament creation narrative to
be pointing to a condition of subordination of women to men, not
only after the Fall, but prior to the Fall, thus belonging to the
order of creation. 1 Corinthians 11 is seen by some of us to
point to a proper, acceptable and right relationship of
subordination that belongs to the created order. Such
subordination was never meant to imply superiority or inferiority.
Indeed there is a proper subordination within the Godhead in the
ordered relationship between the Father who begets the Son and who
sends the Son, and the Son who is the Begotten and the Sent (cf
para. 86). Paul is upholding a right subordination of women to
men. At the same time Paul insists that although woman was first
'made out of man', ever after that man comes to be 'through a
woman': women thus have their own characteristic dignity.
Mutuality and a complementarity of hierarchy and subordination
belong to the created order and not enmity and destructive
hierarchy. Moreover, Paul is not implying in the passage that
women have no public role in the Christian congregation. Indeed,
in the light of his own Jewish upbringing it is surprising that
Paul does not forbid women to speak and prophesy. They must,
however, cover their heads in public. For the sake of seemliness
and order Paul is concerned that when women do speak or prophesy
they should keep their heads covered. In doing so they affirm

56

their womanly dignity,and coupled with that dignity, the characteristic authority that belongs to them as women. At the same time the covering of the head reflects their relationship to men and the authority and headship of men over women. Some of us recognise a **proper subordination** of woman to man upheld in this passage. As man's headship images the headship of Christ over the Church, it is inappropriate, indeed, contrary to the will of God, for a woman (at least within the Christian community), to be in a position of headship or leadership, reflecting Christ's Headship. **For some of us this text is strong testimony against the ordination of women to a ministry which involves, as being a priest does in the Church of England, a headship/leadership role.**

97   Others of us cannot accept the traditional interpretations of 1 Corinthians 11.2-16. They question, on several grounds, the view that Paul's intention was to insist upon the 'hierarchical' leadership of men over women. For example, the idea of a descending hierarchical order in verse 3 is weakened by the uncertainty surrounding the correct meaning and application of the term kephale and the fact that the word is capable of being translated as 'source' or 'origin'. But even if kephale is still best translated as 'head', this need not necessarily denote 'one of superior rank who rules over his subordinates' - unless the rest of the passage were to endorse such a view, which some of us maintain it does not. Again, the way in which Paul's intention is interpreted is affected by the meaning and application of the term exousia. This is translated as 'veil' in the RSV and 'sign of authority' in the NEB. The most natural translation of the Greek term is in fact 'authority' - as the occurrences of the word elsewhere in the Pauline letters indicate (e.g. 1. Cor. 15.24; 2 Cor. 10.8; 2 Cor. 13.10; Rom. 13.1ff). Those of us who question the traditional interpretation of this passage can find no plausible reason why in I Corinthians 11.10 Paul would have used

the word <u>exousia</u>, authority, if he intended to teach Christian
women to wear a veil at worship to denote their subordination to
men. Rather, the word seems to refer to the proper authority a
woman has to speak and prophesy in the redeemed community.
Moreover, there is doubt whether Paul was writing about 'veiling'
or the arrangement of hair during worship. The usual Greek word
for 'veil' nowhere occurs and since verse 15 already refers to
long hair it seems most likely that Paul was requiring Christian
women to arrange their hair in a manner which was not suggestive
of disorderliness or sexual immorality, such as occurred in some
pagan cults. There remains the issue of the use made of Genesis.
In 1 Corinthians 11.7 Paul appears to make a distinction between
man and woman which is not found in Genesis 1.26ff but which was
part of the popular Jewish interpretation of Paul's day: the
contrast between the sexes as to <u>doxa</u>, 'glory', the glory and
image of God being confined to men. Once it has been appreciated
that this was a common notion in Paul's day, it makes sense to say
that, far from endorsing the popular view that women share only
indirectly in the image of God, the Apostle refers to it, and,
having quoted it, proceeded to refute it. In verses 11-12 - which
is not in parenthesis in the Greek but is the apex of Paul's
argument - he stresses the interdependence of men and women 'in
the Lord'. On this interpretation it is the complementarity and
mutuality of men and women which Paul intended to emphasise not
headship and subordination. It could be said that the
presumptions of later translators and commentators about women's
subordination may have influenced their interpretation of this
passage for example in determining their translation of <u>exousia</u> as
'veil' instead of 'authority'. **Those of us who question the
traditional interpretation cannot ourselves find in this passage
from 1 Corinthians anything that forbids the ordination of women
in our own day.**

98   There are others of us who believe that the meaning of the text is indeed that Paul believed that man was the source (kephale) from which woman came. And, since man came first, it followed for Paul that man is indeed predominant. Moreover, since woman was made out of him it follows she is secondary and subordinate to him. Women ought therefore to cover their heads as a mark of subordination to men. The text represents Paul's own view, the popular view of the first century. Paul's view, however, was based on a false premise, no longer admissible in light of modern scientific knowledge about evolution. Those who argue thus hold that Paul was encouraged to draw theological conclusions from what they hold to be false premises, because of the cultural assumptions of his own day. **However today, with our scientific knowledge about evolution and with our different cultural assumptions, based to some extent upon human sciences, some of us do not believe such a passage can any longer be determinative for our view of the relationship of the sexes nor can it determine whether women should be ordained to the priesthood.**

99   There are then some of us who believe that 1 Corinthians 11.2-16 with its teaching on the subordination of women militates against the ordination of women. Others of us feel that the original meaning of the text is by no means clear enough to settle the argument one way or another. There are some others of us who acknowledge that Paul's teaching here is clear. The Apostle is in fact putting forward as his own view, the view of Jewish interpretation of the first century based upon current cultural assumptions namely that women are subordinate to men. However they do not consider that this can decide the matter for the twentieth century question of the ordination of women to the priesthood. Today's scientific knowledge and cultural assumptions are different and Paul was not himself faced with the question of the ordination of women.

(ii) 1 Corinthians 14.33 - 36

100   Whatever view is taken of 1 Corinthians 11, Paul appears to
have accepted that women were in fact legitimately speaking and
prophesying in public.   Verses 23 and 26 of 1 Corinthians 14,
however, would seem to contradict that view:

> As in all congregations of God's people, women should not
> address the meeting.   They have no licence to speak, but
> should keep their place as the law directs.* If there is
> something they want to know, they can ask their own
> husbands at home.   It is a shocking thing that a woman
> should address the congregation 1 Cor. 14.34-35 NEB).
> *RSV reads, but should be subordinate, as even the law
> says.

101   One solution to the problem of apparent inconsistency
between the sentiments of this text and the earlier one is to
regard the passage as a later, non-Pauline, interpolation.   While
there is indeed some awkwardness about the connection between
verses 33 and 34 these are not sufficiently strong grounds for
taking the passage to be an interpolation.

102   The passage raises many questions: does the verb 'to speak'
mean to speak officially or merely to chatter and gossip? - is the
injunction intended only for married women or do all women come
under its strictures? - what is the 'law' to which the author
refers for support?   By 'law' the passage can hardly refer to the
story of creation before the Fall in the Old Testament, at least
not for those of us who see subordination as a consequence of the
Fall and not a part of the created order (Gen. 4.16).   One
solution would be to see a distinction being made between public
prophesying and prophesying within the context of the official
worship of the congregation.

103   We are not all agreed on either the most likely
interpretation of the passage, or its significance to our current
debate. Some of us see this passage pointing, as the earlier
passage, to Paul's understanding of a proper subordination of
women to men as part of the created order, which has to be
reflected in the ministry of the community. While women may speak
in public they may not take a lead in the official worship of the
Christian assembly. Others of us see the overall thrust of the
passage as directed to good order in the community. No one should
violate the communities' rules of order. Certainly, as in
rabbinic Judaism of the time, a woman must avoid questioning
either her own husband or another woman's husband in public.
These verses represent a piece of specific advice given to certain
Corinthian Christians whose behaviour had created a problem. They
are not a general statement about women's subordination and
women's role in the ministry of the community. For some of us the
passage has a particular significance for the debate on the
ordination of women, for others it does not.

(iii) 2 Corinthians 11.3 and 1 Timothy 2.11 - 15

104   At first sight 2 Corinthians 11 and 1 Timothy 2 appear to be
preaching the greater vulnerability of women:

> But as the serpent in his cunning seduced Eve, I am
> afraid that your thoughts may be corrupted and you may
> lose your single-hearted devotion to Christ (2 Cor. 11.3
> NEB)

> A woman must be a learner, listening quietly and with due
> submission. I do not permit a woman to be a teacher, nor
> must women domineer over men; she should be quiet. For
> Adam was created first, and Eve afterwards; and it was
> not Adam who was deceived; it was the woman who, yielding
> to deception fell into sin. Yet she will be saved
> through motherhood - if only women continue in faith,
> love and holiness, with a sober mind (1 Tim. 2.11-14
> NEB).

Both passages refer back to the story of the Fall in Genesis 3.
The story of Eve's deception, tempted by the serpent, was a
popular one in Jewish literature in the early centuries: the blame
for the Fall was unquestioningly placed upon Eve. It is not
surprising that the New Testament writers turned to this vivid
story for illustration. The point made in these two passages
however is not identical. In Corinthians Paul is using Eve as a
type of all humanity: men and women show no difference in their
propensity to be led astray. As Adam is the figure of all, so Eve
also is the prototype for both men and women. The passage is not
commenting upon women as such but upon the whole of the Christian
community. The passage in 1 Timothy is complicated. The verses
appear to be saying that women should be quiet and submissive,
though admittedly it does not make clear whether they are to be
submissive in relation to male teachers, to husbands or to all
men. Moreover, women are not to teach or to have authority over
men. Paul's teaching here is certainly consistent with the view
of the Jewish teaching current at the time. Women are the ones
who, like Eve, yield to temptation and are, therefore, unsuited to
public office. But although women do have a propensity to sin,
yet if women fulfil their God-given role in childbearing they also
may be saved.

105   What seems at first sight to be the most obvious meaning of
1 Timothy 2 is in fact not the only possible interpretation. Some
scholars argue that another interpretation is possible when the
context of the whole Epistle is considered and when the social
background of life in Ephesus in the first century is in view.
Paul is specifically talking here to the wealthy women of Ephesus.
He is dealing with a specific problem of the need for submission
of the wealthy women not to their husbands, but rather to the
teachers of the Christian community. The wealthy women,
undermining the teaching of the faith, are to submit to those who

62

teach the truth. Moreover, those subversive women and not women
in general, Paul is saying, should not have authority over men in
the Church. Further, he uses the story of Eve as a cautionary
tale for the women of his own day and as a positive type of those
who bear children in order to further their own salvation. If
such a line of interpretation of 1 Timothy 2 is taken there is
nothing here to prevent women holding authority within the
Christian community.

106   Some of us would argue, as they did in the case of I
Corinthians 11.2-16, that Paul is once more basing his statement
on the relationship of men to women upon a premise that we should
not longer be comfortable in using today. His premise is that the
serpent beguiled Eve, the weaker partner, and that Eve was the
first to succumb to temptation and proceeded to persuade the man
to sin. Paul based his estimate of the difference of men and
women upon an ancient story whose view of things, as it has been
traditionally interpreted, few people would any longer accept:
namely that women are more inclined to sin than men. While Paul
used this to support his argument that women ought not to be in
positions of authority in the Church in his day, such an argument
can no longer be credibly used. The New Testament is clear that
all have sinned and fallen short of the glory of God: women are no
more inclined to sin than men. As in the case of the passage from
1 Corinthians 11, whatever its instructions for the Church of the
first century, the instruction is no longer relevant for us today.
It is no longer plausible to argue for women to be quiet and
submissive on the basis of their greater propensity to sin.

107   Once more we do not agree upon the implications of these
texts for our subject. Some of us believe that the traditional
interpretation of the texts is right and that they do indeed
reinforce the view that women should be submissive to men and

therefore ought not to be in positions of authority in the Church. They thus militate against the ordination of women to the episcopate and presbyterate. Others of us believe that this is not the only, nor most likely, interpretation of the text. Others among us do not believe that the matter of the ordination of women can be settled by reference to such texts whatever their original meaning for the Church of the first century. They hold the argument to be based on a premise no longer acceptable today.

Ephesians 5.21 - 33 and 1 Corinthians 7

108   In describing relationships transformed by Christ the writer of Ephesians 5 turns to the relationship of husband and wife. A general injunction 'Be subject to one another out of reverence for Christ' is followed by:

> Wives, be subject to your husbands, as to the Lord; for the man is the head of the woman, just as Christ also is the head of the church. Christ is, indeed, the Saviour of the body; but just as the church is subject to Christ, so must women be to their husbands in everything (Eph. 5.22-24 NEB).

Some of us regard it as significant that the writer of Ephesians 5 is not only speaking of the marriage relationship here but that he also refers to a more general principle of a submission of women to men which belongs to the created order. In the Christian community the pattern and image for the relationship of a man and a woman is the relationship of Christ to the Church. Christ is the Head of the Church, his body: so man is head of woman. While the author is not directly addressing the question of ministry in the Church, the passage nevertheless has important implications for the question of the ordination of women to the priesthood. It suggests that women ought not to be in a position of authority/headship, over men. Moreover, for some of us, as Christ is Head of the Church, it is appropriate that only men should

64

image the headship of Christ, for men are in the order of creation head over women. As Christ is the Bridegroom, the Church the Bride, it is appropriate that men should represent Christ in the ordered ministry. (Here we are back to the argument of who may appropriately represent Christ to the Church, an argument we considered in paras 49-67 of Chapter 2).

109 Others of us, while agreeing that the author of Ephesians has accepted the prevailing pattern of male authority accepted in his own day, believe the importance of the passage does not lie so much in the re-affirmation of the principle of submission. What is of primary significance is the way that pattern is re-formed by the writer. The writer does not deny the authority of man over woman but gives a new vision of the way that relationship is to be lived out. The submission of a woman to her husband, the love of a husband for his wife, are to be lived out as Christ lived for the Church: he gave himself up for the Church; he nourishes and cherishes it. That is the model of the love husbands are to show their wives; the model of submission wives are to show to their husbands. The quality is the same whether in loving, or in submitting: it is mutual. 'Be subject to one another out of reverence for Christ.' **Some of us believe that the passage ought not to be used to uphold the subordination of women to men as a general principle. Moreover, it does not have a direct bearing on the question of the ordination of women to the priesthood, a question not being asked or answered by the writer of Ephesians 5. What is important is what the passage says about the quality of human relationships, in particular the quality of relationship that befits husband and wife.**

110 In the context of the Corinthian correspondence, it is clear that Paul's teaching about male-female relations in 1 Corinthians 7 is directed to a specific situation. (cf 7.1: 'Now concerning

65

the matters about which you wrote...') The principle enunciated in
v 4 is given in response to questions about the marriage
relationship and not to modern formulations of questions about the
ordination of women to the priesthood. Nevertheless it is
important to balance the teaching set out here with other biblical
passages which do not seem to suggest that Christian women should
have any kind of authority over men. In the first clause in v 4,
Paul appears to take up the theme of the words addressed to the
woman in Genesis 3.16: 'Your desire shall be for your husband, and
he shall rule over you'. The Apostle goes on to offset this
dictum with the striking assertion that 'the husband does not rule
over his own body, but the wife does'. Some of us would discern
here a notable contrast between the disharmonised relationships of
'fallen' men and women before the coming of Christ and those
within the community of the redeemed. Others would favour a more
limited interpretation, whilst acknowledging the fact that Paul
describes conjugal rights as reciprocal.

111   One further text in particular is much used in the debate on
the ordination of women and deserves examination.

Galatians 3.27

> For through faith you are all sons of God in union with
> Christ Jesus. Baptized into union with him, you have all
> put on Christ as a garment. There is no such thing as
> Jew and Greek, slave and free man, male and female; for
> you are all one person in Christ Jesus (Gal.3.26-27 NEB).

112   In the Epistle to the Galatians Paul is exploring and
contrasting life under the law and life under promise. Uppermost
in his thought is the division between Jew and Gentile. However,
in this passage he refers to three pairs that formed the three
deepest divisions in his own day. They were the three divisions
familiar to a Jew who thanked God each morning that he was neither
a Gentile, a slave, or a woman. What Paul is saying is that none

66

of these differences which split society ought to be cause of division within the baptised community - Paul is not denying difference but claiming that difference ought not to be a cause of division. In his writings Paul works this out for the division of Jew and Gentile but never in the same detail for slave and free, or man and woman. It would be odd, however, if, as in the case of Jew and Gentile, Paul believed that there were no practical consequences, no changes in behaviour and custom, relating to the other two divisions. Indeed, it is possible that in other places he does hint at reforms needed, though he never provides a comprehensive reform programme. As we have seen, Paul affirmed women as co-workers; he accepted that, contrary to Jewish practice, a woman might prophesy and speak in public; he proclaimed a mutuality in sexual relations, the wife's body belongs to her husband, a husband's body to his wife. Those of us who take the view that Paul endorses a male headship would also readily agree that Paul is concerned to set relationships between men and women in a baptismal context which has reforming consequences in the life of the Christian community. However, the principle laid down in Galatians 3.27 is not worked out by Paul for the many questions facing the Church and society of his own day, neither does it meet the questions facing the Church in the twentieth century. It is, however, relevant to look at our contemporary question about the ordination of women in the light of the Pauline principle set out in Galatians 3.27. **What significance for the Church (as it faces the question of the ordination of women to the priesthood) has the Pauline principle that in Christ there is neither male nor female? For some of us the principle is supportive of women's ordination: for others of us the passage is primarily relevant in a baptismal context and other biblical passages have a greater relevance for the question of the ordination of women.**

113   Whatever our differences so far we are all agreed that what
we have said has also to be set in a much wider perspective of
biblical teaching. We are all impressed by the attitude of Jesus
to women in his own ministry. He did not adopt the Jewish
attitudes and customs of his day. Women were among his close
friends accompanying him on his journeys through Palestine; he
discussed religion with a woman at a well when there was no one
around; he healed a woman unclean because of the loss of blood; he
shared meals with women, numbering prostitutes amongst his
friends; he allowed a woman to wipe his feet with her hair and
another woman to anoint his head with precious oil. There was no
woman amongst the Twelve and yet Jesus first entrusted the news of
his resurrection to women telling them to go and proclaim the
message to the male disciples. The women were there at his birth,
at the foot of the cross and in the garden at his resurrection.
**We are all agreed that the Gospel record of Jesus' relationship to
women is remarkable when set against the patriarchal customs of
Judaism of the day. Nevertheless there are those of us who do not
believe that the argument used against the ordination of women
which rests upon the fact that Jesus did not appoint women to be
apostles can be lightly dismissed. If it is dismissed it raises
the question of what authority can be given to any of our Lord's
actions and words,if he were so constrained by his environment.
For others of us, while the New Testament witness to Jesus'
attitude to women does not directly support the ordination of
women, it seems to point significantly in that direction.**

114   When set against the undeniably patriarchal society of the
first century, we are all impressed by the positions that some
women held in the early Christian communities. In Acts there is
Tabitha, a prominent disciple in Joppa; Lydia, Paul's first
convert in Europe, who had her whole household baptised; the four
daughters of Philip the deacon who 'possessed the gift of

prophecy'; Phoebe in Romans 16.1 is called a deacon; Priscilla according to Acts 18 is seen as a teacher; in Philippians Euodia and Syntyche share Paul's struggles. All of these references to the roles women played in the life of the early Church form a background to understanding the specific Pauline texts about women looked at earlier.

115 Neither Jesus' attitude to women nor the references to women in the life of the early Church directly support the ordination of women to the priesthood; nevertheless they seem to many of us to point significantly in that direction.

(iv) Summary

116 As we have worked together at the biblical material relating to headship and authority we have discovered, as with the issue of representation and priesthood, that there is much upon which we all agree: the goodness of the male-female relationship in creation; men and women, both created in the image of God, are made for each other to live supporting and loving one another; sexuality is a part of God's good creation; sin has the power to distort and destroy the relationship of communion between the sexes as it distorts the relationship between groups and races; in the community of the baptised there can be no room for division between the sexes, any more than between Jew and Gentile; difference is not obliterated but is no longer a cause of division; in spite of the patriarchal society of the first century Jesus numbered women amongst his close companions and women came to hold important positions in the life of the early church; the Gospel called for a radical critique of the relationship between the sexes in the first century and stands in judgement on the distortions of that relationship which have continued throughout history.

69

117 On all of this we are agreed. We are not agreed, however, on whether there is a proper subordination belonging to the created order and a distinctive authority of man over woman. Some of us believe that both the Old and the New Testaments are consistent in upholding the view that women are subordinate to men and that there is an authority of men over women that stems from the order of creation. Those of us who believe this hold that this is the message of Genesis 2, and a message reiterated in the teaching of Paul as seen, for example, in 1 Corinthians 11 and 14 and 1 Timothy 2. The biblical view of women's subordination is not, as was later thought by Aquinas, because the weaker members must be governed by the wiser; nor is it because man is more rational than woman; nor because women are inferior. It is rather that for harmony and stability in life one person must depend upon another for direction. In exercising authority men are characteristically men and in being subject to authority women are characteristically women. This difference in function is built into the order of creation. Subordination is a positive gift in creation: exercised with the mutuality of love it reflects order within the Godhead. The principle is to be lived out most clearly within the marriage bond: a man is to be head over his wife and head over the family, but 'the husband must give his wife what is due to her and the wife equally must give the husband his due' (1 Cor. 7.3). This proper combination of subordination and mutuality is to be reflected also in the community: it is not a curse but rather a blessing. It signifies that there are things which properly belong to one sex and not to the other. Once this principle is acknowledged, some of us believe it follows that priesthood may be one of those things: one aspect of complementarity is that men may properly be priests while women may not. This is balanced by the fact that, for instance, women can be mothers while men cannot. Complementarity does not mean

70

interchangeability. **Those of us who hold this view of headship, subordination and complementarity** hold that women ought not to be ordained to a priesthood which entails leadership, oversight, headship and the exercise of authority. To so ordain women would be to contradict a fundamental creation ordinance.

118 More of us, however, believe that the biblical passages, both Old and New Testament, are most concerned with asserting the equal status and dignity of women and men. The dominant conviction of the Genesis texts is that men and women are of the same nature and were made for unity and communion. This comes over in spite of the patriarchal culture in which the texts were formed. Only through the Fall does man become domineering, woman subservient. Paul, struggling in the patriarchal context of his day, is at pains to refute the popular distorted view of women as inferior to men, more inclined to sin and less in the image of God. Paul is concerned to re-form the contemporary view in the direction of mutual submission in love and equality between the sexes. Paul's view, for some of us, is affirmative of women although he never fully works this out for every area of the Church's life, nor entirely frees himself from the views of his own day. It is consonant with Jesus' own treatment and affirmation of women. Neither Old nor New Testament presents a systematic treatment of the mutuality between the sexes; nevertheless there are those of us who are most impressed by the biblical witness to the equality of status of women and men created and redeemed in the image of God. To continue to preclude women from being ordained priests in this generation damages the Christian witness to the world to the equality and status of women and men created in the image of God. The unity of humanity, an essential aspect of God's good creation, is also obscured. **Those of us who believe that the Bible does contain pointers to support the ordination of women to the priesthood do not hold that**

complementarity between the sexes is to be worked out on the basis
of the assignment of the different orders of ministry to women and
men. Complementarity ought rather to be reflected in the
character and style in which all ministry is exercised.

119 Finally, there are some of us who are less sure about the
thrust of biblical teaching. They cannot find any clear or direct
guidance on the question of the subordination of women to men and
men's headship over women. Even where a biblical passage appears
to be putting forward a view of subordination, as in the case of 1
Corinthians 11, it is not sufficient to argue that that message is
determinative for today. The Old Testament and the New Testament
writers were not faced with our questions and they use premises
which we are no longer happy to base arguments upon. Hence the
question of the ordination of women to the priesthood cannot be
settled simply on the grounds that Scripture either precludes such
ordination or demands it. The matter has to be settled on other
grounds than Scripture. **If all other reservations were to be met,
such as the question of the unity of the churches, or internal
Anglican unity, there are those of us who consider that Holy
Scripture would not preclude such a step. According to this view
its witness is not so obvious that it compels the Church to move
in that direction before other obstacles have been overcome.**

Chapter 4

PRIESTHOOD, THE UNITY OF THE CHURCH, AND THE AUTHORITY OF THE ORDAINED MINISTRY

120   In the two previous chapters we set out the reasons why we differ on whether women should or should not be ordained to the priesthood. Those reasons relate to priesthood and representation, and the views some of us have about the headship of man over woman. We attempted to set out divergent views in the context of much shared agreement on the nature of priesthood, the sacramentality of the ministry and the goodness of sexual differentiation. When we turn to the issue of **the priesthood, the unity of the Church and the authority of the ordained ministry** we discover once again that our disagreements lie within a broader context of much that we hold in common.

121   Unity and communion belong to the very nature of the Church. The inner fellowship or communion of the Church is grounded in the life of God the Holy Trinity. This inner communion and unity of the Church is maintained and manifested in the visible life of the Church. The ordained ministry of the Church is an instrumental sign of the Church's communion. This is well expressed in the following:

> By the express will of Christ the Church is called to be one; so too is its ministry. Just as baptism by incorporating believers into Christ makes them members of the whole Church, so too ordination by setting particular persons aside as ministers of Christ, makes them bishops or presbyters of the whole Church. The disunity of the people of God imposes limitations on the exercise of the ordained ministry in the universal Church; but these do not remove its essentially universal character. This link between the universality or catholicity of the Church and the universality of its ordained ministry makes the mutual recognition of ministry a matter of central concern in the quest for

Christian unity. For the Church cannot be seen to be one unless its ordained ministry is seen to be one, nor indeed can Christ himself be seen to be one unless those who are appointed to act in his name are at unity with one another (12).

The quotation rightly emphasises the relationship between the unity of the Church and the ordained ministry.

122   The ordained ministry has a particular responsibility for maintaining and focussing the Church's unity. For one Church to be in communion with another involves recognition of all their baptised members as members of a single community of faith: it also involves mutual recognition of those who are called to be ministers of the communion of faith and love, particularly in its eucharistic celebration.   In the episcopal churches the bishop has a special ministry for safeguarding the unity and continuity of the Church both locally and universally.   A bishop represents the Christian community in his diocese to the wider Church and the wider Church to his diocese.   A bishop exercises his ministry particularly in conjunction with his presbyters and deacons. While the recognition of ministries and the communion between all the ordained is necessary for maintaining the communion of the Church, the episcopal ministry is of particular importance both for maintaining and focussing communion.   Non-recognition and rejection of episcopal ministry would, therefore, seem to be even more damaging of communion than non-recognition of presbyters (13).

123   Ecclesial unity and the unity of the ministry is however to be seen within the context of that fuller unity to which Christ calls us, the unity of a redeemed humanity.   The Church as a reconciled community, and its ministry, are called to be a credible sign to the world of that unity that is God's purpose and God's design for all creation. **Whatever view each of us holds**

about the ordination of women we all share a deep concern for the unity of the Church and the importance of the unity of the Church for the Church's mission. Concern for the unity of the Church and for the mission of the Church have to be held together: they ought not to be played off against each other.

(i) The Ordination of Women, the Unity of the Church, and the Unity of the Kingdom

124 The preceding understanding of the relationship between the unity and communion of the Church and the ordained ministry leads some of us to believe that it would be wrong to ordain someone as a priest whose ministry could not be recognised by all in one Province, by the Anglican Communion as a whole, or, some of us would argue, by the wider ecumenical fellowship, particularly by those Churches which have retained the threefold catholic order. Such a step would damage, or further damage, one of the bonds that hold the Church together. Indeed the ordination of women to the priesthood in some Provinces of the Anglican Communion has already impaired the ecclesial fellowship of the Anglican Communion. We no longer have a fully interchangeable ministry. Non-recognition of ministers within the Church of England would further impair Christian unity. Some of us believe that the ministry would be even less serviceable as an effective sign and instrument of unity.

125 To ordain women to the presbyterate within the Church of England at this time would have a detrimental effect on the moves towards Christian unity. Some of us believe it would be theologically wrong. Baptism, Eucharist and Ministry makes it quite clear that there is no consensus, not even convergence, on this issue in the broadest ecumenical context represented by the Churches which are members of the Faith and Order Commission of

the World Council of Churches (14). The <u>Ministry Text</u> includes a carefully balanced statement of the opinions of those who favour ordaining women and those who remain opposed. Our international theological dialogues with both the Orthodox and Roman Catholic Churches show the difficulties both these large Communions would have were the Church of England to follow other Provinces of the Anglican Communion in ordaining women. The position of the Archbishop of Canterbury within the Anglican Communion adds a further complicating dimension to the Church of England's decision.

126   In his letter to the Archbishop of Canterbury in 1984 Pope John Paul II described the ordination of women as 'an increasingly serious obstacle' to progress towards reconciliation between our two Communions. Nevertheless, 'obstacles do not destroy mutual commitment to a search for reconciliation'. In a subsequent letter to the Archbishop of Canterbury, Cardinal Willebrands referred to the progress made between our two Churches and went on:

> our greater unity must be a fundamental concern, and it has to be stated frankly that a development like the ordination of women does nothing to deepen the communion between us and weakens the the communion that currently exists. The ecclesiological implications are serious (15).

127   Some of us believe that were the Church of England to ordain women as priests this would further put at risk further our Anglican growth in unity with the Roman Catholic Church, at least in the foreseeable future, and thus hinder the progress towards the wider recognition of the ministry of the universal Church. However illogical it may seem, action by the Church of England appears to have about it a significance, even finality, for some Churches, that action by other Provinces of the Anglican Communion has not. Any action by the Church of England to proceed to ordain women ought at the very least to await the work of ARCIC II. The

Commission has the task of continuing the work already begun on ministry and, in particular, has been asked 'to study all that hinders the mutual recognition of the ministries of our Communions'. Some of us are concerned that once a division of this sort has been created between our two Communions without an understanding being first reached the situation becomes polarised: it becomes much more difficult for agreement ever to be reached. In assessing the effect on ecclesial unity some of us believe that the divisive effect of the ordination of women to the priesthood in the USA, in Canada and in Sweden has been seriously underestimated: attention must be given to that. Further, the experience of Lutherans and of Free Churches which have not maintained the threefold ministry cannot be unequivocally applied to our situation.

128 There are some of us who remain opposed to the ordination of women on theological grounds and who believe only a truly ecumenical consensus has sufficient authority to make such a radical change. There are others of us who feel, because of ecumenical advance, that the time is inopportune. More widespread ecumenical consultation is needed and more demonstrable convergence shown on the issue before the Church of England ought to decide to proceed to ordain women.

129 Many of us, however, believe that the ordination of women should not wait upon its recognition either by the whole Anglican Communion or by the Roman Catholic and Orthodox Churches. To them it is encouraging that there is a growing number of Provinces in the Anglican Communion that do now ordain women and many affirmations are made of the blessings that ministry has brought to the life of those Provinces. It is also important that the Roman Catholic Church has not broken off theological discussions with the Anglican Communion in spite of the fact that some

Provinces have ordained women. What happens in the Church of
England is not decisive for the whole of the Anglican Communion,
or for the relations of the Anglican Communion with other
Churches. Further, encouragement can be taken from the statement
by Pope John Paul II that 'obstacles do not destroy mutual
commitment to the search for reconciliation'. It may prove
possible to move into deeper communion in spite of a diversity of
practice on the question of the ordination of women. To insist on
waiting for a time when the ordination of women may be accepted by
the Orthodox and the Roman Catholic Churches would in fact mean
deferring action, as far as can be judged, almost indefinitely.
It is encouraging that during the recent visit of the Ecumenical
Patriarch, Demetrios I, to the Archbishop of Canterbury it was
announced in their official Joint Communique that a Pan-Orthodox
Symposium will be held in 1988 to articulate the doctrinal reasons
for the maintenance of the Orthodox position against the
ordination of women to the priesthood. Documentation of Anglican
discussions for and against the ordination of women was also
requested as background material for the Symposium and this House
of Bishops Report will itself be part of such material. In
addition the practice and counsel of the Lutheran Church and those
Free Churches which already ordain women need to be taken
seriously.

130   Not to proceed to ordain women to the priesthood might, some
of us believe, hinder our growth into unity with the Free Churches
certainly at the local level here in England. In our dialogue with
the Reformed Churches, the ordination of women is seen as
integrally related to the life together in unity of Christians at
the local level. God's Reign and Our Unity suggests that 'it is
clearly impossible for churches which exist in the same
geographical area but which take different stands on this issue to
enter into complete union' (16).

78

131   The ordained ministry is a sign and instrument of communion
in the universal Church and is thus closely related to the
Church's vocation to be a credible sign of the kingdom in a
divided world.   The kind of communion and unity the ministry is
called to exhibit is to point to the coming kingdom and be a sign
of what human community, redeemed in Christ, can be like. **Some of
us, therefore, believe that to have an ordained ministry, in any
one of its three orders, which is only male, is an incomplete sign
of true unity that belongs to men and women created in the image
of God.** The risk of either impairing the unity of the Provinces of
Canterbury and York, or the wider Anglican Communion, or of
reinforcing already existing divisions in Christendom ought not to
be considered of greater importance than the more adequate and
convincing sign of unity which a truly comprehensive presbyterate
and episcopate would give.   The symbol of an all-male episcopate
and priesthood carries with it negative and destructive overtones.
The effect of the symbol is to reinforce deep hurts and alienation
within the Church and within society.   Some women and men thus
find it hard to see the Church as a community of liberty and
reconciliation, and a pointer to that unity in Christ in whom
there is neither male nor female. This has a detrimental effect
upon the mission of the Church in some parts of the world.

132   The risk of impairing the unity and communion of the
Anglican Communion, or of reinforcing divisions between existing
Christian denominations, has therefore to be weighed against what
some of us see as the greater risk of failing to be a sign to the
world of the depth of true unity and communion. It is for this
reason that some Provinces of the Communion argue that the mission
of the Church in their own country demands not only the ordination
of women to the presbyterate, but also to the episcopate.   The
bishops of the Church of Canada, for example, in their submission

79

to the Primates' Working Group on women and the episcopate quoted the following resolution passed by the Canadian House of Bishops. The Bishops:

> (3) In recognising that the episcopate is a sign of unity, note the importance of Lambeth discussions on the consecration of women as bishops within our Communion both so that the unity of our Communion may be maintained and so that the fullness of God's gift in men and women may be received within the episcopate to the creation of a deeper unity and a more effective witness in the carrying out of our mission (17).

133   Some of us then are not persuaded by the argument that women ought not to be ordained until their ministry can be recognised by the whole Anglican Communion and by the Roman Catholic and Orthodox Churches. A major development in the teaching and life of the Church may need to be acted upon by some before it is received, or indeed accepted, by the whole Church. Councils were sometimes a way of responding to already well advanced developments and disputes rather than a way of setting out a theoretical line of advance into previously unexplored areas, (for a longer discussion of reception c.f. Chapter 6). Some of us therefore believe that far from being divisive, an inclusive ministry in the Church of England would be a powerful witness to the depths of unity that we are seeking in the ecumenical movement. Those of us who hold this view recognise that it represents a different view of unity than was articulated in some union negotiations. However, they regard it as a richer and deeper view of unity.

134   **Whatever our view on the rightness of proceeding to ordain women, we have all come to recognise in our discussion about the relationship between the priesthood and the unity of the Church that the differences are not between those of us who believe passionately in maintaining the unity of the Church and those who have no regard for unity. There are those of us who sincerely**

believe that the unity of the Church, and the potential moves to
unity in the current ecumenical movement, would be threatened by
such action. Some of us are convinced that it would be
inopportune to take the step at present. Others of us hold that
the depths of unity and communion in Christ will be more fully
realised and visibly expressed when women bring their different
but complementary gifts to the exercise of priesthood. The
reconciling message of the Gospel will be more audible to the
world through the sign of an inclusive ministry. Whatever side of
the debate we are on we all share a concern for unity, the unity
of the Church and the unity of the Kingdom.

(ii) The Ordination of Women and the Authority of Ministry Exercised in the One, Holy, Catholic and Apostolic Church

135   There is a further and closely related issue which concerns
the ordination of women and the authority of ministry exercised in
the One, Holy, Catholic and Apostolic Church. Those ordained are
ministers of Christ in his Church. Theologically, this means
that, in intention they are ministers of the One Christ in his One
Body, the One Church. Anglicans have consistently claimed to have
continued the ministry of the universal Church. This is witnessed
in the retention at the Reformation of a threefold ministry.
Although the scandal of Church division subverts the sign of the
universal ministry, Anglicans have never ceased to uphold this
universal claim for their ministry. Canonical restrictions limit
the exercise of ministry but this does not affect the claim that
bishops, priests and deacons are not ministers merely in the
Church of England but bishops, priests and deacons in the Church
of God. Thus, to ordain someone involves a claim for a
potentially universal ministry. This has its parallel in baptism:
individuals are baptised into the Church of God and not into a
particular denominational expression of the Church. Baptism

conveys membership of the Church of Christ; ordination ministry in the universal Church.

136   One intention of ordination is to show beyond doubt that the person so ordained has authority to exercise the office and work of a priest in the Church of God. We are all agreed therefore that it is a grave step to ordain someone knowing that their ministry is less likely to be recognised or to be acceptable as authoritative, either within a single Province, or within the Anglican Communion or in the wider ecumenical fellowship. So to ordain a woman would involve the creation of an element of division, or at least serve to reinforce divisions that already exist. To ordain a woman to the priesthood in the Church of England at this time would certainly mean that the authority of her ministry would not be recognised by some parishes and dioceses in England or by some Provinces of the Anglican Communion.

137   It is arguable that to ordain women to the presbyterate would have a further detrimental effect on the potential for growth into unity with the Roman Catholic Church and the Orthodox Churches and thus put back the recognition of ministries in the foreseeable future. Although the declaration of Pope Leo XIII that Anglican Orders are 'absolutely null and void' still stands, there is nevertheless 'substantial agreement' on the understanding of ministry and priesthood expressed in The Final Report of ARCIC: and there is a confidence that this agreement may form the basis for a recognition of ministries in the not too distant future. This confidence ought not to ignore the fact that the ordination of women is regarded as a 'grave obstacle' to the reconciliation of ministries.

138   **There are, then, those among us who would argue against the Church of England ordaining women as priests unless such**

ordinations are recognised by the whole Anglican Communion and by a much greater proportion of the wider ecumenical fellowship. Unless there is wide recognition of women's ordination, particularly by those Churches which have themselves retained the historic episcopate, to ordain women would be to reinforce old divisions and erect new divisions and to put in question even further the authority of the ministry of the women so ordained.

139   While we all recognise that it is a grave matter to ordain someone whose orders will not be regarded as belonging to the universal ministry, we also all recognise that it is similarly a grave matter to reject the ministry of any person who is intentionally ordained to the universal ministry. This is at present the case with those who are unable, in all conscience, to recognise the orders of women lawfully ordained abroad.   Such a lack of recognition also impairs the unity of the Church and weakens the authority of the ministry.

140   There are some of us who are unable in any circumstances to recognise the orders of women priests described as 'lawfully ordained abroad'. Some others of us who are able to acknowledge their priesthood nevertheless believe that every Province should be given space and freedom to consider the matter in the process of forming its own mind.   Thus the ministry of women priests ought not to be forced upon any Province ahead of a formal decision by the Province concerned.   In living out a proper balance between the autonomy and interdependence of the Provinces of the Anglican Communion, some of us believe it is appropriate for a Province to proceed unilaterally and for other Provinces to request that a women lawfully ordained abroad should not exercise her ministry in another Province until that Province has declared its own mind. The respecting of different views is a mark of interdependence.

141 We are, then, all agreed on the importance of the question
of the relationship between the priesthood, the unity of the
Church, and the authority of the ordained ministry. We disagree
however on the implication of this for the Church of England's
decision on whether or not to ordain women to the priesthood.
There are those of us who remain opposed to the ordination of
women and think it wrong on theological grounds. Nor, some of us
believe, has the Church of England the authority to make such a
decision which would be damaging to the unity of the Church and
limit even further the recognition of ministries. Others of us
feel that while the time may come in the future for such a step to
be taken, it is at present inopportune. However, many members of
the House of Bishops believe that there are positive reasons for
proceeding now to an inclusive ministry for the sake of the Church
being a more credible sign of that unity and communion which
belong to the kingdom. This would enhance the role of the ministry
both as a sign of unity and authority and strengthen the Church's
witness in mission.

Chapter 5

THE CHURCH'S SOURCES OF AUTHORITY FOR DISCERNMENT AND THEIR USE

142   In the preceding chapters we set out three areas we believe
to be central in the current debate on the ordination of women:
priesthood and representation; priesthood, headship and the
exercise of authority; and priesthood and the unity of the Church
and the authority of the ministry.   In determining the relevance
each of these issues has for the question of the ordination of
women to the priesthood, constant reference was made to the
witness of Scripture, the Church's tradition and contemporary
experience.   It is the characteristically Anglican way of forming
a mind on matters of faith or order to be guided by the Scriptures
in the light of tradition, reason and experience.

143   Answers to contemporary questions can be successfully
formulated only from within the community of the Church which
encounters and passes on the tradition of the Gospel in its
worship, thought and conduct.   We all affirm that questioning is a
necessary part of Christian discipleship: there is place in the
life of the Church for both tradition, enquiry and even conflict.
Provided that the questioning is undertaken with faith in God who
promises to lead us into all truth, with dependence upon the Holy
Spirit and with a forbearance towards those whose views differ
from our own it will never be hurtful (18).

(i) The Bible

144   New insights about the truth of the Gospel and the life of
the Church under the Gospel proceed from the interplay between
that which the Church has received from the past and that which it

experiences and reflects upon in the present. This interplay is
like a conversation between, on the one hand, the historic
revelation received and handed on by the Church, and, on the
other, all the constantly changing observations and thoughts which
need to be related to that revelation (19). The present debate on
the ordination of women is part of the perpetual conversation that
goes on in the life of the Church and will go on as long as the
Church exists in an attempt to remain faithful to the truth of the
Gospel and to make the Gospel audible and credible in every age.

145   In this conversation the Bible has a unique place. As
Article VI of the 39 Articles puts it, the Scriptures contain all
that is necessary to salvation. This is because Holy Scripture is
the unique revelation of the nature and activity of God and of
God's purposes for his people. In Jesus Christ God has achieved
his decisive and determinative act. Every authentic Christian
life depends on sharing by faith in the fruits of that act of God
in Christ. Every authentic Christian vision is controlled by it.
What God has given at the start in Christ has an authority and an
authoritativeness which must have no rival in its control over us,
if the Church is to continue to be the community, sign and servant
of God's salvation for the world (20).

146   The Bible has 'controlling authority' in the life of the
Church because in it, and through it, we receive the first witness
to Jesus Christ, the first reactions to his life and teaching, his
death and resurrection in ways which both bring out God's purposes
in those events and evoke a response of faith. The Old Testament
contains the unique witness to God's self-revelation in creation
and history, and to the building up in a covenant relationship
with himself of the community into which Jesus was born and grew
up. The Old Testament helps us to understand who Jesus was and
the message his disciples proclaimed concerning him. The New

86

Testament writers convey the teaching of Jesus Christ and, with a wide range of concepts and insights, the early Church's response to him, and his work; they explore the imperatives of faith for human living, and wrestle in the Spirit with the mystery of the goal which, in and through Christ, God has in store for his creation. 'The Scriptures, both Old and New, must always have a controlling authority. We need to place ourselves continually under the Scriptures if we are to draw on the grace of that truth of God which brings salvation, and to grow in Christlikeness'(21).

147   We all agree that the Bible is our primary and normative source possessing 'a controlling authority'. At the same time the Scriptures do not easily yield a ready-made answer on all matters relating to faith, order or morals. The task of using the Bible to determine an answer to such questions often involves complex exploration. The obvious meaning of a biblical text may be obscured by linguistic difficulties; the relation of a passage to its particular context and position in the canon not immediately clear; there may be doubt about the message the text was intended to convey in the particular cultural context in which it was first spoken; and the meaning of an individual passage has to be seen in the light of the overall message of the Bible for Scripture interprets Scripture. Even when a message is clear for the community for which it was written the gap has to be bridged between the original context and today, the two horizons: we have to ask what message a particular teaching or custom conveys in very different conditions from when it was first given and whether that same message needs to be couched in different language, symbols and imagery. In the case of slavery, for example, the custom of slavery stands alongside the biblical witness to the equality and dignity of every human being. It took centuries and changes in society, for the consequences of the Gospel to be seen for the practice of slavery. On the other hand a custom or

institution may be changed contrary to the values of the Gospel, as some would uphold has happened in relation to marriage and divorce.

148   While we are all agreed on the sovereign authority of Scripture and the controlling place it must have in the life and decisions of the Church, and in our individual lives, we recognise at the same time that using the Scriptures is not always as straightforward as a confession that Scripture has a controlling authority may sometimes make it appear. Chapter 3 of this Report demonstrates something of what is involved in using the Bible for guidance on the question of the ordination of women to the priesthood. We found we were not always of one mind in our understanding of the original meaning of some passages crucial for our debate. While some of us, for example, found the original meaning of some of the Pauline texts clear, others of us had questions about the precise meaning of the original Greek text: this in some instances rendered a different meaning possible. Even when we did all agree on the meaning of a text we were not always of one mind on what message that text was conveying to the community for which it was written, living in a very different cultural context from our own. When we came to apply the message to our own day we were forced to ask how best that message might be conveyed in a world with very different assumptions and customs. Moreover, when we came to sum up the overall biblical teaching on the nature of men and women and their relationship to one another we again found different emphases amongst us. This was particularly evident in what we hold to be the biblical teaching about the subordination of women to men and the headship of man over woman and the outworking of that in the life and ordering of the early Christian community. We also found ourselves taking issue with one another over the significance of the maleness of Jesus in the incarnation and its relation to the

self-revelation of God in the whole of the biblical witness.
**Whatever our differences over the interpretation of Scripture, we
acknowledge that those of us who argue for continuing an all male
priesthood and those of us who argue for an inclusive priesthood**
believe their view to be **consonant with Holy Scripture and not**
contrary to its message.

(ii) The Tradition

149   In attempting to form our mind on contemporary questions we
read Scripture in the light of the Church's tradition. Scripture
is the normative, primary and controlling source of authority. The
tradition of the Gospel has been, and goes on being, handed on in
the worship and thought and life of the Church. Tradition is not
a second witness or an additional source of information to
Scripture: it is, rather, an expression of the life of the Holy
Spirit in the Church, the living continuity in which the Church,
guided by the Holy Spirit, has interpreted its message through the
ages. Tradition is not an ever accumulating hoard of static
material. It is living and dynamic: 'it is that within which
Christians live, pray and worship' (22). This view of a dynamic
tradition is entirely in keeping with Scripture's work as the
living Word.

150   Anglicans have always given importance to the formative
period of the Church, the period of the Fathers, the Creeds, the
early liturgies, ministerial order with its all male priesthood,
and the great Ecumenical Councils. But ever since the split
between East and West, and until our own day, the tradition of the
Church has been handed on, and lived out, in the separated
traditions of the different Churches. On many matters, whether of
faith or order, there is agreement among all the main Christian
Churches and appeal can be made to the historic tradition of the

Church. However, on other matters, as in the case of the ordination of women to the priesthood, different convictions and practices have come to be held and lived between, and even within, a single denomination. Some of us would want to claim that the traditions of those Churches which have retained the threefold order with an all male priesthood carry particular weight for them, especially when seeking guidance on a matter which concerns the ministry of the universal Church. Others of us believe that the development in some Churches in opening the ministry of Word and Sacrament to women is a prophetic witness.

151   When the question of the ordination of women to the priesthood is set in the context of the Church's tradition it is hardly surprising that many people are impressed by the fact that for almost two thousand years the Church has continued an all male priesthood. But just as there has to be a hermeneutic of Scripture so also must there be of tradition. We need to ask what the tradition of an all male priesthood was proclaiming in the various cultural contexts of the Church's history. Only then, as in the case of Scripture, can we turn to our own day with its very different assumptions and patterns of life and ask, does that practice or doctrine still say to us now what it intended to say to the Church then? Does it help the Church to proclaim the Gospel or does it in fact prevent the message of reconciliation being heard?

152   For much of the past history of the Church the prevailing view of men and women emphasised the differences between the sexes, and society was built upon quite distinct and rigid role patterns and expectations for women and men. The primary role for all women was seen as supporter of her husband, bearer of children and nurturer of the family. Women were not expected, or encouraged, to take their place in society outside the home except

in serving and supportive roles. Education for women was rare and the professions not open to them. For many the roles and expectations of women were linked to a powerful, and now well documented, tradition which saw women as defective males, only in the image of God when joined with a man. All of this clearly had an effect upon the relationships, roles and status of men and women in society, but also in the Church, not least of all in the leadership of the Church. Some of us, however, want to stress also that not all past views of the relationship between the sexes were discriminatory in character. The Bible and the continuing tradition contained a view which held women in high regard and recognised them as equally in the image of God. In spite of this positive view of women there was no challenge made until now to an all male priesthood. For some of us this is an important argument for the Church's continuation of an all male priesthood.

153   We have to set side by side with the long history of an all male priesthood the fact that there have been women who have exercised a ministry as confessors, teachers, theologians and, increasingly since the last century, as missionaries. Despite the fact that women could not be ordained there are examples of women abbesses who were mitred, given staff and ring, authorised to hear confessions, described as <u>sacerdotes</u> and granted, for a period, ecclesiastical and civil authority. And, since the middle of the last century in the Church of England, women have increasingly experienced a call to minister in the name of the Church, a ministry which has been recognised and accredited. The order of deaconesses was revived in the 1860s by Bishop Tait, then Bishop of London. More recently the third order, the diaconate, has been open to women in many Provinces of the Anglican Communion, including the Church of England. In this case the Church of England felt able to take a step affecting the universal ministry without seeking explicit authorisation of the whole Church. (Some

of us would wish to make clear that in agreeing to the ordination
of women to the diaconate, while still opposing the ordination of
women to the priesthood, they did so on the grounds that tradition
does not exclude it: indeed the witness of the earliest tradition
indicates that in the early Church the diaconate included women).
In addition to the increasing role for women in the Anglican
Church, ministries for women are opening up in the modern Roman
Catholic Church, especially, but not exclusively, for members of
religious orders. Many of the Free Churches as well as the
Lutheran Churches have already admitted women to a full ministry
of Word and Sacrament.

154   We all believe that the tradition of the Church is living
and dynamic and that the Church is called upon to proclaim the
faith afresh in each generation (23). The past provides more than
precise terminology or fixed forms of order: it provides
'inspiration and guidance under God' who in his saving purpose is
always making all things new. What is brought to each generation
is the grace and truth of Christ which is more than fixed
formularies and structures (24). Development has always been a
characteristic of the Church's tradition. The Church has changed
its mind upon a number of matters as on both slavery and usury.
On the question of the ordination of women we differ in our
estimate of what guidance the tradition gives us. **There are those
of us who believe that the unbroken tradition of an all male
priesthood is not a failure to make the Church and its ministry
appropriate in particular cultural contexts. They believe that a
male priesthood was, and still is, a way of safeguarding and
proclaiming important and vital truths which are to be found both
in creation and revelation which tradition must preserve in the
redeemed community. Those of us who maintain this rejoice in the
developing official ministries for women, including the opening up
of the diaconate to women. This is a right expression of the**

92

complementarity of women's ministry in the Church. Such special accredited and ordained ministries (in the case of the diaconate) are to be exercised in partnership with men in the presbyterate and episcopate. For many others of us, however, the tradition of an all male priesthood for hundreds of years was, in part, the consequence of the Church's response to its environment. Those of us who hold this view see the more recent developments in recognised ministries of the Church for women, especially the opening of the diaconate to women, as pointing towards the admission of women to the priesthood and episcopate. Others of us, as in our estimate of Scripture, remain agnostic on the significance of the Church's tradition. It is not that they believe development on this matter would be wrong; they simply do not know.

(iii) Present Experience

155   We began the chapter by agreeing that new insights about the truth of the Gospel and the life of the Church under the Gospel proceed from an interplay between that which the Church has received from the past and that which it experiences and reflects upon in the present. Religion never stands still. It is in an interplay of Scripture and tradition on the one hand and experience on the other, that new insights emerge. In order to grasp the truth of Holy Scripture and of the Church's continuing interpretation of Scripture in tradition, we use the God-given and God-directed gift of reason. By reason we understand our capacity as individuals, and our corporate capacity as a Christian community, to reflect upon Scripture and tradition. But reason is more than that. It also includes the capacity to use our God-given power of thought to grow in understanding our experience of life, of nature, of our contemporary history and to bring that experience into living interaction with Scripture and tradition.

93

Scripture and tradition sometimes confirm what is happening in the contemporary situation, saying 'yes' to what is new and radical. Scripture and tradition also have the power to judge and condemn contemporary experience and say 'no' to change. God's word is heard, his guidance found in the creative interaction between what is going on in the Church and the world, and what has so far been understood, believed and practised in the tradition of the Church.

156   The biblical teaching on women and men created in God's image and the ordering of the life and ministry of the early Church developed in a very different world from that in which we live in the West today. The last one hundred years have seen a revolution taking place in the role and status of women in society. Women now have the vote, all major professions (apart from certain orders of the Church's ministry) are open to them and women take a greater part in forming decisions which affect their own lives. A review of the newspapers in the last twelve months would show, however, that the process of reform is by no means complete. And the recent Church of England Report Servants of the Lord, chaired by Dr Margaret Hewitt, leaving aside the question of women and priesthood, calls for reforms in the life of the Church of England in respect of the participation of women (25). The Sex Discrimination Act and the existence of the Equal Opportunities Commission have improved the position of women in employment although there remains evidence of continuing discrimination against women sometimes in overt, more often in hidden ways. A vocal and articulate women's movement has emerged both outside the Church and inside the Church dedicated to redressing a perceived imbalance perpetuated by a society in which dominant forms of thought and expression are understood to be determined by, and reflect, the needs of men and where the needs and experience of women are forgotten, ignored or, at best, subsumed under categories created by and appropriate to men (26). However, the

94

growing movement of women, and women and men together seeking for a renewed community of women and men in the Church in organisations like Women in Theology, the Movement for the Ordination of Women, the Catholic Women's Network, the Christian Women's Resource Centre and the International Ecumenical Decade for Women has not gone unchallenged. The recently formed Women Against the Ordination of Women and other similar groups, reveals a different vision for the outworking of the complementarity of the sexes in the life of the Church. Many women and men however still remain altogether untouched by the claims of either reforming movement.

157   The opening of the diaconate to women in recent years in the Church of England as well as in other Provinces of the Anglican Communion has been an important step in the development of the ministry of women in the Anglican Communion. Not all of us, however, see this as a move towards the opening up of the priesthood and the episcopate to women. It is not an innovation. Indeed, the witness of the earliest tradition indicates that there were women deacons in the early Church. Moreover, examination of the history of the ministry of women in the diaconate makes it clear that the Church has felt able to use, adapt and develop it, even to discard it or allow it to lapse, in response to the needs of the community, ecclesial or secular, in which it finds itself; and in so doing it did not feel the need to refer to Churches of other places or times for justification. It was, however, some of us believe, precisely the fact that women admitted to the diaconate were not thereby set on the path to priesthood or episcopacy, were not incorporated into the male 'career structure' of ministry, that made this flexibility possible. There are those of us who hold that the re-opening of the diaconate to women is fully acceptable: it does not involve women in a ministry of oversight and leadership (cf para. 20). Many of us, however,

95

regard this step as an important one on the way to the ordination of women to the priesthood. They are impressed by the fact that many of the women now serving as deacons believe themselves to be called to a priestly ministry.

158 A part of contemporary experience of particular relevance to the debate on the ordination of women to the priesthood is the testimony of many women that they feel a vocation to priesthood and request that the Church at least put to the test their conviction of being called (27). The request is not primarily about claiming rights for women, equal rights with men in the public institution of the Church. Some of us however believe that the question of justice cannot be divorced from the debate. The stories are mostly of women who, against all the odds, have experienced, often slowly and painfully, a growing sense that God is calling them to the priestly ministry. Often that call is interpreted in the only way the Church makes possible, a call to lay ministry or, more recently, to minister as a deacon. Often it is only after ministering to communities as lay women that women come to understand their call as a call to a full sacramental priestly ministry. Some women have come to believe that their ministry is being thwarted by their not being able to preside at the eucharist, or pronounce an authoritative word of absolution to those to whom they have been giving counsel, or not being able to exercise oversight in the communities to which they minister. The concern of many women is not limited to the functions of priesthood but to the denial of their very priesthood which affects both them and those to whom they minister. There is another side of these stories which reflects and confirms the experience of many women. This is echoed in the stories told by those who receive the ministry of women in the already recognised ministries of the Church. 'While the Church argues whether women should or should not be ordained, it has already happened in this

parish.' It is not simply that women grow in understanding their call to priesthood divorced from the Christian community but that the Spirit, through the local community, appears to some of us to be calling forth a priestly ministry in women. Some of us, therefore, believe that the Church of England should now move to put that sense of vocation to the test.

159   There is also the considerable experience of women in priesthood in other Provinces of the Anglican Communion that forms part of the contemporary experience relevant to the debate. In his letter to Cardinal Willebrands, the Archbishop of Canterbury acknowledged that although 'deep division...even to the extent of tensions which strain the bonds of communion' exist in some of those Provinces yet every such Province indicated that its experience was beneficial and none had been led to abandon the development (28). The more recently published Report of the Primates' Working Group on Women and the Episcopate contains reflections from a number of Provinces about their experience of women in the presbyterate. Those reflections are positive, while also revealing that division over this matter still remains in some areas (29).

160   While many see the experience of women as pointing in the direction of the Spirit calling the Church of England at least to test the vocation of women to the priesthood, it also needs to be acknowledged that there are many in the Church of England, and within and outside the Anglican Communion, also seeking to be guided by the Spirit, who have a deep conviction that the ministry of the ordained priesthood is not God's will for women in the Church. This is the case even amongst some people who have experienced the priesthood of women. In all Provinces which do ordain women there are those who continue to be opposed to such ordinations and who remain within their dioceses with varying

degrees of marginalisation. Others have felt no longer able to remain within the Anglican Communion.

161   In our search for an answer to the question whether we should proceed to ordain women to the priesthood we have attempted to listen together to what God is saying to the Church, in and through the contemporary world and through the Church's present experience. And we have tried to ask what we can make of our experience in the light of Scripture and tradition and what that experience itself says to Scripture and tradition. We have considered what our continuing practice of an all male priesthood says to the Church and the world. Does the continuation of an all male priesthood make evident in our own day the truth of the Gospel we have received, or does it in England in the twentieth century obscure the truth of the Gospel handed down to us?

(iv) Where the Process of Discernment Has Led Us

162   There are those of us who believe that by continuing to ordain only men to the priesthood the Church of England will remain most faithful to the long tradition of the Church and continue to bear witness to the truth of the Gospel in our generation. An all male priesthood will witness to those things about the nature and being of God which were signified in the particularity of Jesus' maleness: a male priesthood will continue most faithfully to represent the priesthood of Christ in the sacramental life of the Church; it will point to the role and status of men in relation to women according to the purposes of God in creation and redemption, by testifying to the headship of men over women and the proper subordination of women to men. Those of us who hold this view believe this to be an important witness to our society as men and women struggle to find new patterns of relationship and new roles for women. Further, an all

98

male priesthood will continue to be a powerful witness to the continuity of the Church's ministry from the time of the Apostles till today, and a link with the Roman Catholic, Eastern Orthodox and Old Catholic Churches, and thus be important for the continuity, the unity and the communion of the Church.

163   Others of us, however, believe that the continuation of an exclusively male priestly ministry in twentieth century England actually obscures the truth of the Gospel. They believe that the insights and the experiences of the society around us stand in judgement upon our continuing exclusive practice. The persistence of an all male priesthood threatens our mission and our unity. The symbol of an all male priesthood no longer makes evident to the world what we believe about the unity and communion of men and women in creation and in the kingdom. The symbol of an exclusive ministry, some of us believe, reinforces patterns of inequality and alienation which make it difficult for many women (real and particular women), and some men, to belong to the Church. Those of us who hold this believe that it makes it hard for the world to recognise the Church as a community of liberty and reconciliation (30). An inclusive ministry, they believe, would point beyond human divisions towards the equality and dignity of women and men created in God's image and point the world to the communion of the kingdom. Further, they believe that an inclusive ministry would proclaim more fully truths about God the Holy Trinity - the God who is neither male nor female, in whom those qualities we call masculine and feminine are encompassed and transcended in the wholeness of divine life and love. An inclusive ministry would witness in our fragmented world that the Church is the place where the kingdom is being born, where the Holy Spirit breaks down the barriers that divide, breathes new life, heals and restores. Moreover a fully inclusive ministry will bring a greater wholeness as both male and female experience is brought to the deliberations

99

and decisions of those who exercise oversight as bishops, or delegated oversight as presbyters. Those of us who are convinced that the Church of England should proceed to ordain women to the priesthood acknowledge that this may slow down the movement into deeper fellowship with some Churches, notably the Roman Catholic Church and the Orthodox Churches, but they cannot put the concern for ecclesial unity above that unity which they believe the values of the Kingdom of God demand. Those of us who are in favour of women's ordination believe that it is a way of communicating in our day the faith of the Gospel without losing its essential character: it is a way of proclaiming afresh the truth of the Gospel. Some of us believe that while it is time to ordain women to the priesthood restraint should be exercised in relation to the episcopate.

164   Others of us are more cautious.   They cannot find anything in Scripture or tradition which settles the matter conclusively one way or another: neither does the experience of the Church today make the matter clear for them.   They remain agnostic and are inclined to believe that the time is not right to make such a move, which they believe would put strains upon the Church of England and be detrimental to our unity with other Churches.   Yet others of us believe that the evidence points to the rightness of an inclusive ministry in time but they do not believe that that time has arrived.

165   The decision over the ordination of women has to be taken by the Church discovering the will of God through the work of the Holy Spirit under the guidance of Scripture and in the light of tradition, reason and experience.   We have tried to show how in our work on the question of women's ordination we have used the sources of Christian authority. An answer to the question cannot be given by expert theologians, by any pressure group, or even by

the bishops apart from the Church. It is our responsibility as
bishops to guard the tradition, to guide the Church, to care for
the unity and fellowship of the Church and to seek to comfort
those who will be hurt by whatever decision is reached and acted
upon. But the decision has to be taken by discerning the mind of
the whole Church. And so we turn in the next chapter to the
process of decision making when there is division in the universal
Church.

Chapter 6

THE PROCESS OF DECISION MAKING WHEN THERE IS DIVISION
IN THE UNIVERSAL CHURCH

(i) The Decision-Making Process

166   In Chapter 5 of our Report we set out the sources of
authority that Anglicans use in forming a decision on questions of
faith or order or morals. The decision on the ordination of women
to the priesthood has to be made by the Church under the guidance
of the Holy Spirit, a decision grounded in the Holy Scripture, and
made in the light of the living tradition of the Church.

167   **There are those of us who believe that the consensus of the
whole Church is vital to express the true assessment of the
respective parts played by Scripture, tradition and reason. Until
such time as the whole Church has declared its mind, their
understanding of the unique role of Scripture and its particular
message in relation to the question of the ordination of women
leads them to remain opposed to such action. It is, they believe,
inadmissible for a single Province of the Anglican Communion, or
indeed the whole Anglican Communion, to take a decision on a
matter which affects the unity of the Church and involves a
change, or at least significant development, in the universal
ministry. A decision ought, therefore, to wait until it can be
taken in the fellowship of all the Churches in a fully ecumenical
council.** Some of us who put this argument see the need for some
kind of representative conciliar gatherings ahead of a truly
ecumenical council, in which issues that affect the unity of the
Church, like the ordination of women, might be considered. The
meeting of Primates in Washington in 1981 reflected that

> In a divided universal Church, the Anglican episcopate
> shares its peculiar responsibility with those called and
> chosen to exercise episcope - the totality of Christ's
> Church. The Anglican episcopate acknowledges that it has
> a special obligation to consult with leaders of other
> Churches and thereby to practise collegiality in a
> divided Church.

This tacit acknowledgement that Anglican bishops are unable to exercise their collegiality in isolation imposes strict limits on the authority of even a world-wide Anglican Communion, let alone a merely national or General Synod.

168   We all recognise that Anglicans are in the process of reflecting about the structures of authority and decision making within the Anglican Communion. Just at a time when we are being made to think about structures of authority and decision making in response to the Final Report of ARCIC, and the implications of the Lima Text with its reference to 'personal, collegial and communal' ministry exercised at every level of the Church's life, we are faced with a question concerning the ministry of the universal Church. It might seem that we need those questions of authority answered, and answered not only in the abstract but embodied in our life, before we can proceed to settle the question of women's ordination. There are those of us who doubt whether it is realistic, or indeed right, to defer taking a decision on a question so pressing as the ordination of women until such time as there are universal structures in place for common decision making.

169   The structures of decision making within the Anglican Communion have developed and are still in a process of developing: so too are the structures of consultation which exist between Anglicans and other Churches. One of the important characteristics of the Anglican Communion is the tension that exists between the autonomy of the Provinces and their

interdependence. While episcopal guidance can be expressed through the Lambeth Conference, effective decisions at present can be taken only at Provincial level. Regard ought to be taken by an individual Province for the views of the Anglican Communion, expressed particularly by the Lambeth Conference but also by the Anglican Consultative Council and the Primates' Meeting, all of which seek to preserve the interdependence and unity of the Anglican Communion. However, some are beginning to recognise that there is a problem to be faced in reconciling the idea of Provincial autonomy with voting at the Lambeth Conference. Such voting does not give equal weight to the decisions of individual Provinces. In forming a mind Anglicans need also to take account of the views of other Churches and a proper concern shown for our growing into unity with those Churches.

170 **Many of us, while acknowledging the integral relation between the ordination of women and the unity of the Church and the universal ministry, believe that a decision on the matter cannot be deferred to some indefinite future: it must be made, using faithfully the structures of authority and decision making that do currently exist. The matter is of such concern that a decision ought not to be deferred indefinitely. The failure of another Church to reform itself ought not to be a reason for the Church of England failing to act on the will of God as they perceive it.**

171 Those of us who consider that a decision on the matter ought not to be postponed believe that if the Church of England decides to ordain women, on the basis of the current theological discussion, that decision will have been taken with responsible consultation and with due regard for the interdependence of the Provinces of the Anglican Communion. And, moreover, in the absence of any ecumenical council, Anglicans have consulted widely on the

subject in bilateral and multilateral dialogues. The <u>Lima Text</u>
sets out the current state of the debate in a carefully worded
commentary in the <u>Ministry Text;</u> the Anglican-Reformed Dialogue
<u>God's Reign and Our Unity</u> has an explicit statement about the
ordination of women; and more recently a consultation of the
United and Uniting Churches, including Churches Anglicans are in
full communion with, spoke with gratitude of the witness of those
Churches which have ordained women to Word and Sacraments and who
have found it a 'creative element in their common life' (31). The
correspondence between the Archbishop of Canterbury, the Pope and
Cardinal Willebrands shows as does the work of ARCIC I and II,
that Anglicans have been particularly anxious to discuss the
matter with the Roman Catholic Church, and the subject has been
raised in the Anglican-Orthodox dialogue. Further, those of us in
favour of the procedures now taking place believe that any
decision of the Church of England to proceed to ordain women would
be consonant with the resolutions of the Lambeth Conference of
1978 which recognised

> the autonomy of its member Churches, acknowledging the
> legal right of each Church to make its own decision about
> the appropriateness of admitting women to Holy Orders
> (32).

172   The Resolution makes clear that 'the holding together of
diversity within a unity of faith and worship is part of the
Anglican heritage'. The Conference stated 'that those who have
taken part in ordinations of women to the priesthood believe that
these ordinations have been into the historic ministry of the
Church as the Anglican Communion has received it'. The intention
behind the Lambeth Resolution was not to make a definitive
judgement for the Anglican Communion on the validity of such
ordinations but to respect the positions of both sides. In
Resolution 21 the Conference

(a)   declares its acceptance of those member Churches which now ordain women, and urges that they respect the convictions of those provinces and dioceses which do not;

(b)   declares its acceptance of those member Churches which do not ordain women, and urges that they respect the convictions of those provinces and diocese, which do.

As a result some bishops leaving the Lambeth Conference thought that the question of the validity of such ordinations had been settled: others thought it had not been settled. However, no bishop present at the Conference said that the ordination of women to the priesthood was an issue which should lead to a break of communion. We all recognise, however, that difficulties have arisen because insufficient attention was given to the question of how such Resolutions of the bishops were to be received and the possible effect on the reciprocity of ministries within our Communion which would ensue. One of the characteristic signs of a breach in communion is the refusal to recognise ministry. The refusal of the Church of England to allow women lawfully ordained abroad to celebrate in this country on the basis of their sex alone, and the refusal of some male priests and bishops from Canada and the USA to celebrate when visiting this country, have impaired our communion. We are not out of communion with other Provinces but steps have been taken on both sides which 'unmake' ecclesial communion.

(ii) Reception

173   The last twenty years have seen the recovery of the concept of reception. Attention has been given to the question how conciliar statements were received in the life of the early Church. And reception has come to the centre of the ecumenical discussion in relation to the way in which the fruits of ecumenical dialogues, like the Lima Text and the Final Report of ARCIC, are received in the life of the Churches. In the early

Church it was recognised that Councils can err and that the reception of conciliar resolutions by the churches and by the people of the Church is important. In the case of the admission of the Gentiles to the Church and the matter of circumcision, Paul's actions as part of the expanding Church were in advance of the decisions of the whole Church. However, before this was determined to be right it had to be agreed by the 'Apostles, Elders and the whole Church' (Acts 15). Reception is not passive obedience to conciliar statements but a living process in which church leaders, together with the faithful, respond and receive into their lives the insights of a council. The process is an open one: there is the possibility of the acceptance or indeed of rejection of a conciliar statement. In an open process of reception there is always the possibility that what is being tested will wither and die. But the reception process itself does not confer validity on a statement, it affirms and acknowledges it. If, in the course of time, the Church as a whole receives a conciliar decision, this would be an additional or final sign that it may be judged to be in accordance with God's will for the Church (34).

174 Whenever a matter is tested by the Church there is necessarily an openness about the question. The continuing communion of Christians with one another in faith and worship maintains the underlying unity of the Church while the reception process is at work. The openness needs to be recognised and accepted by those on both sides of the debate. There needs to be openness to the possibility of the new thing being accepted by the Church or rejected by the Church. It also entails a willingness to live with diversity throughout the 'reception' process.

> Reception is a long range and far reaching process in
> which the whole Church seeks to recognise and affirm
> confidently the one faith... and confidently to lay hold
> of the new life which that faith promises (35).

175   We all recognise that there is a very particular problem
when what is being tested in the reception process is not just a
doctrine to be discussed but a doctrine that is embodied in
persons, and, more especially, embodied in the ordered ministry
which effects an essential bond of communion of the Church. There
is thus a 'facticity' about what is being put to the test of
reception. Where the Church's order is concerned, the process of
reception may thus mean an impairing of communion while the open
process of reception takes its course. Any impairing of communion
is a painful process and it is the local church that is likely to
experience it most acutely: what is tolerable between Provinces
is increasingly difficult between dioceses or parishes within the
same geographical area. This is particularly so in the parochial
system of the Church of England. While we all recognise the
difficulties in submitting the ordination of women to an open
process of reception the possibility remains of continuing in a
communion of faith, life and witness on the basis of carefully
worked out safeguards. We all recognise that any such process
will put particular strains on those women who are ordained to the
priesthood and whose ministry appears in question in a way that
does not apply to men.

176   **In spite of the difficulties many of us have come to
recognise the significance of the place of reception in the matter
of the ordination of women.** They believe that the continuing
fellowship of Anglicans with one another in faith and sacramental
fellowship by the grace of God will protect the underlying unity
of our Communion while the reception process is at work. If, as a
result of these debates, the Church of England decides to proceed
with the ordination of women, its decision will not be contrary to
the guidance of the bishops of the entire Communion as set forth
in the resolutions of the 1978 Lambeth Conference. That decision

will still have to be tested in the dioceses of the Church of England. In the course of such testing, sensitivity to those who remain opposed is essential. And care needs to be expressed through detailed safeguards to ensure that people are not forced to accept the ministrations of a woman against their conscience.

177 Even if the reception process is completed by the Church of England, the decision still has to be accepted by the entire Anglican Communion and indeed by the universal Church before it can be deemed to be the mind of Christ for his Church. We note that the recent Report of the Primates of the Anglican Communion on <u>Women and the Episcopate</u>, which also discussed the notion of reception in relation to the ordination of women to be episcopate,describes the current situation within the Anglican Communion in regard to the open process of reception already in process on women and priesthood. Those Provinces which have already ordained women speak positively of their experience. There is also a willingness to listen to the experience of Provinces which for a variety of reasons, theological and cultural, have not proceeded to ordain women. The evidence supports the view of the Archbishop of Canterbury summed up in his letter to Cardinal Willebrands:

> I must also say something of the experience of those Anglican Churches which have taken the step of admitting women to the ministerial priesthood. While honesty compels me to acknowledge deep division on this matter amongst Anglicans - even to the extent of tensions which strain the bonds of communion, those Provinces which have taken this step have indicated to me that their experience has been generally beneficial. Nor have they yet heard compelling arguments to abandon this development. It is also possible that some other Provinces of the Anglican Communion will take similar decisions in their respective Synods.

109

(iii) Summary

178   There are some of us who continue to believe that neither a single Province within the Anglican Communion, nor indeed the Anglican Communion acting together, possesses the authority to sanction such a development or change in the universal ministry as would be the ordination of women to the priesthood. They consider that the Resolution passed at Lambeth 1978 was unwise but perhaps it was inevitable in that no consideration was given to the question how the Church would live with the situation that would ensue. It has served to further dissension within the Anglican Communion; implicit in the Resolution, of the autonomy of individual Provinces to make up their own mind on the question of the ordination of women was a decision hastily taken and did not represent a considered theological judgement. Some of us feel that the decision placed more weight upon the principle of the autonomy of Provinces than on the interdependence of the Anglican Communion. Furthermore no thought was given to the way in which the Resolutions might be received. All of this has led to a serious impairing of communion which they believe would be escalated should the Church of England proceed to ordain women. They remain opposed to the ordination of women to the priesthood on theological grounds.

179   Many of us, however, believe that notwithstanding the present state of division in the universal Church it is proper for the Church of England to take a decision on the question of the ordination of women to the priesthood, and to act upon that decision. This is the only way in which such a decision can at present be taken within the Anglican Communion. They consider that appropriate guidance has been given by the bishops in the Resolutions of the Lambeth Conference, that adequate appropriate consultation has already taken place with the Provinces of the

Communion, and with other Churches. However, they believe it important that any such move on the part of the Church of England would need to be tested in an open process of reception - within the Church of England, the Anglican Communion and the wider fellowship of the Churches. In that process care must always be taken to safeguard the consciences of those who remain opposed.

180 **Others of us who cannot find any theological objections to women's ordination to the priesthood nevertheless continue to hold that the time is inopportune.** Some of us are worried about the effect it would have on the Church of England at this time. And our commitment to the ecumenical movement, in particular our commitment to the Roman Catholic and Orthodox Churches, leads them to caution restraint. It is not helpful for Anglicans to engage in dialogue with Roman Catholics for the reconciliation of ministries while taking an action in regard to the universal ministry which the Roman Catholic Church has indicated would be a 'grave new obstacle' to reconciliation. There is now indication that the matter is being raised within the Roman Catholic Church by lay men and women, clergy, bishops and theologians. We should wait to see how that debate develops. It may be that dialogue between our two Churches, with discussions in the Anglican-Roman Catholic Commission, would lead eventually to a consensus and a decision which could be authoritative for a much larger part of Catholic Christendom than the Anglican Communion. Some of us hold that, while individual churches may come to a conclusion on the theological issues, these can be determined in a way which would justify action only by an ecumenical consensus. In this matter truth and unity are inseparable.

181 Whichever of these three positions any of us holds we would all encourage as full a discussion of the matter as possible to accompany the present discussion of 'the proposed legislation'.

We hope that careful, charitable and informed discussion will take place at parochial, deanery and diocesan levels, leading to a responsible decision by our Church.

Chapter 7

FINAL REFLECTIONS

182   The earlier chapters of this Report explore the issues that
seem to us to be the crucial ones in the current debate on the
ordination of women to the priesthood. The bishops found that it
was to these issues they kept returning: in each area our
substantial disagreements lie within the context of much that we
hold in common. It has been important for us to affirm together
as much common ground as we are able as well as to clarify the
precise points of our disagreement.

183   The five issues form part of an interlocking agenda. We
cannot get far in discussing priesthood and representation, for
example, without raising questions of authority and headship, the
use of the Bible, and who takes decisions on such matters in a
divided Church. Further it is clear that our answer to the
question of the ordination of women to the priesthood is affected
by what we believe about the ministry, the nature and purpose of
the Church, the significance of sexual differentiation and, not
least of all, by what we believe about the nature and being of
God. While, therefore it is a matter which is integrally related
to what we believe at the level of faith, that does not settle the
question. **For many of us, the ordination of women to the
priesthood would be a legitimate development in accordance with
some of the deepest insights of Scripture and tradition; for
others the change would represent a fundamental, theological
change which would call in question the Church's witness and
obedience to Scripture and tradition.**

184   It is not easy to explore an issue about which people hold
such firm views and which touches things at the centre of our
faith. Moreover, it involves not only what we think but what we
feel. The process of listening to views opposed to our own is
hard. It is important for those who hold differing opinions to
acknowledge the integrity of others. A great deal of patience is
needed in the process of our helping one another to put into words
why we hold our own particular view. However disconcerting and
frustrating it is for some who have rehearsed the arguments, as it
seems, for too many years, the discussion must continue. Whether
the Church of England is to proceed to ordain women, or remain
with an all male priesthood, it is essential that an informed
decision is taken and that as many people as possible are drawn
into the forming of the mind of the Church. We also believe that
should the Church of England proceed to ordain women great care
ought to be taken to safeguard those whose consciences will not
allow them to receive the priestly ministration of women. Although
the General Synod passed a motion in 1975 that there were 'no
fundamental objections' many have said that the earlier vote was
taken with insufficient discussion of the theological issues. This
Report is presented to the General Synod in the hope that it will
serve to stimulate informed theological discussion and to indicate
the sensitive points which in the view of the House of Bishops
require particular attention. The bishops hope that, as the
legislation is considered by the General Synod, and, if given
general approval, by diocesan synods, members of the Church of
England will discuss the issues, complex as they are. A decision
will have to be taken. Whatever the outcome the effect on the
life of the Church will be profound.

We acknowledge that as a House we are not all of one mind.

Many of us believe that the Church of England, after the present consultative process and on the basis of widespread discussion, may take a decision. They are in favour of the Church going ahead now. They nevertheless hold that should women be ordained to the priesthood the matter would still need to be received in the Anglican Communion and in the other Churches.

Others of us do not believe that the Church of England should proceed to ordain women to the priesthood now. They do not, however, share the same reasons for this judgement:

- some of these accept the theological arguments for the ordination of women to the priesthood but believe, for the sake of unity, that a greater consensus should be reached in the Church of England and in the Anglican Communion before such a step is taken.

- others, unconvinced by the other theological arguments either for or against the ordination of women to the priesthood, are persuaded that restraint ought to be exercised by the Church of England in view of the lack of a clear ecumenical consensus at present. This for them is itself a theological argument.

- finally, some of them are opposed on theological grounds in the areas of the authority and interpretation of Scripture, priesthood and representation, and priesthood and headship of man over woman. These areas carry the implication that to ordain women to the priesthood would be a fundamental change to the Church's ministry and therefore not a legitimate development.

Postscript

WOMEN AND THE EPISCOPATE

(i) The Debate So Far

185   The 1978 Lambeth Conference influenced developments in
relation to the ordination of women to the priesthood: it also
contributed to the debate on the ordination of women to the
episcopate. Although, as we said earlier, not all would agree the
wisdom of the Conference Resolutions on the matter, Resolutions 21
and 22 provided some preliminary background for the discussion of
women and the episcopate. Resolution 21 noted that since Lambeth
1968 four Provinces had proceeded to ordain women to the
presbyterate and eight other member Churches of the Communion had
'either agreed or supported in principle or stated that there are
either no fundamental or no theological objections to the
ordination of women to the historic threefold ministry of the
church' (our underlining). This might be thought to suggest that
Resolution 21 in fact envisaged the possibility of ordination to
the episcopate. This would be in line with the view held by some
in the 1970s which assumed that, once women were ordained to the
presbyterate, there were no further arguments to preclude
consecration to the episcopate. However, Resolution 22, devoted
to 'Women and the Episcopate', hinted at an implied difference
between ordination of women to the presbyterate in a Province, and
consecration to the episcopate:

> While recognising that a member Church of the Anglican
> Communion may wish to consecrate a woman to the
> episcopate, and accepting that such a member Church must
> act in accordance with its own constitution, the
> Conference recommends that no decision to consecrate be
> taken without consultation with the episcopate through

116

the Primates and overwhelming support in any member
Church and in the diocese concerned, lest the bishop's
office should become a cause of disunity instead of a
focus of unity (36).

186   Not surprisingly, some of those Provinces which now have ten
or more years, experience of women in the presbyterate, among them
women serving in senior positions as Deans of Cathedrals,
Archdeacons, or Canons, are facing the question of the
consecration of women to the episcopate.   In September 1985 the
House of Bishops of the Episcopal Church in the USA passed a
resolution expressing its intention not to withhold consent to the
election of a bishop on grounds of gender.   At the same time the
House of Bishops remained faithful to Lambeth 1978 and sought the
advice of the episcopate of the Anglican Communion through the
Primates Meeting.

187   At the meeting in March 1986 in Toronto the Primates
welcomed the request of the USA for consultation and saw it as
indicating that the Episcopal Church recognised the consequences
its action would have in the life of the wider Anglican
family - and ecumenically.   The Primates did not see the request
for consultation as a request for permission to go ahead.   Indeed
they were aware that the Episcopal Church had the constitutional
right to proceed to consecrate women to the episcopate.   Nor was
it merely informing the Communion about what was to happen.

> They saw consultation as a two way process in which,
> while the Episcopal Church could explain the reason
> behind its position, the other Churches of the Communion
> could present their reflections on this issue and in
> turn themselves be challenged. Consultation was seen to
> include a spelling out of the consequences of the
> ordination of women to the episcopate within the wider
> Anglican family, in order that the Episcopal Church's
> decision should be as fully informed as possible.

188   We note that more recently, in April 1988, a woman was

117

nominated as a candidate for a new Coadjutor Bishop of Michigan. A woman was also nominated in the diocese of Iowa. In neither case was the candidate elected. Following on the Toronto Meeting the Archbishop of Canterbury set up a small Working Party, under the Chairmanship of the Archbishop of Brisbane, The Most Reverend John Grindrod, with the task of gathering responses of the Provinces to the admission of women to the episcopate.

(ii) Our Response to the Primates' Working Party

189   At the meeting of the House of Bishops in July 1987 we considered the statement of the Toronto Primates' Meeting on <u>Women and the Episcopate</u>. We also had before us unpublished material from a member of the Church of England Working Party set up by the Archbishops of Canterbury and York to study the question of the ordination of women to the episcopate. (The terms of reference of the Cameron Group were subsequently revised to embrace a general study of the episcopate with particular reference to the question of women and the episcopate. This Report is not expected to be published until 1989.) In July 1987 we passed the following resolutions which were sent to the Grindrod Working Party:

> (1)   The House of Bishops welcomes the statement on <u>Women in the Episcopate</u> agreed by the Primates' Meeting, Toronto, March 1986, and endorses its request to the Archbishop of Canterbury for consultation on this matter between the Provinces of the Anglican Communion.
>
> (2)   The House of Bishops recognises the inter-relatedness of the theological issues raised by both the ordination of women to the presbyterate and episcopate, but it also notes that the question of the ordination of women to the episcopate is only likely to become a live issue in a Province if and when that Province has a mature experience of women priests otherwise suitable for consideration for the episcopate.

(3)   The House of Bishops considers that within the theological issues - eg. 'headship' and 'representation' - ecclesiology is especially relevant to any consideration of women in the episcopate; it draws particular attention to para 42 of the House of Bishops' Report The Ordination of Women to the Priesthood (GS 764):

> Although not strictly within our remit, the question of the consecration of women as bishops was seen to be closely related to the ordination of women to the presbyterate and to the considerations relating to that legislation. It is very difficult to sustain an argument for any essential sacramental distinction between the presbyterate and the episcopate such as to put in doubt the possibility of a woman's admission to the episcopate once the presbyterate has been granted. However, on grounds of the authority of jurisdiction which belongs to a bishop and the scriptural issues of headship, some might want to argue against such consecration. Further, because of the ecclesiological role of a bishop as focus of unity within his local Church and his role as symbol and link of communion between his Church and the universal Church, it might be considered by some as inappropriate to consecrate a woman as long as some Provinces remain opposed in principle to the ordination of women. There might be considered sufficient ecclesiological reasons for caution and restraint on the question of the consecration of women to the episcopate while there is no consensus on the issue. While it is possible to legislate in the case of priests diocese by diocese, the episcopate, as bond of unity and communion between dioceses and Provinces, could not be so legislated for. Were bishops not able to recognise each other's ordination and therefore not able to act collegially, that would lead to a serious rupture in communion. We recognised that such considerations are being looked at by the Archbishops' Group on Episcopate.

The House of Bishops went on to encourage the Archbishops' Group on Women and the Episcopate and the Primates' Working Party:

> (a) to continue to explore these issues, together with a consideration of the positive and negative implications of women in the Episcopate for

koinonia within the Anglican Communion, within the
developing ecumenical fellowship, and within the
wider unity of humanity.

(b) to consider how change or development in Order
is received by Anglicans within the universal
Church.

(c) to examine the implications of one Province
admitting women to the episcopate in advance of
other Provinces.

(iii) The Grindrod Report

190   The Grindrod Report Women and the Episcopate, has now been
sent to all bishops of the Anglican Communion to aid discussion in
preparation for the Lambeth Conference in July 1988. The first
part of the Report, 'Listening as a mark of communion', summarises
the reflections from seventeen Provinces on the question of women
and the episcopate. The evidence shows that the Provinces are at
very different points in their thinking on the issue. For some
Provinces the issue is immediate and pressing; for some others it
is hardly on their agenda at all. A range of opinion is
expressed. The Report suggests that 'it is not a simple matter of
those in favour clamouring for immediate action and those against
threatening a rupture in communion and demanding the issue be
dropped. Amongst those against there are some eager for further
discussion and exploration and even a suggestion that it might be
possible to provide pastoral guidelines which would make it
possible for those in favour and those against to remain in
communion.' Amongst those in favour there are differing views on
the appropriate time scale for action. What is clear, however,
from the responses is the value every Province places upon
consultation and listening to other Provinces. There is also a
general acceptance of restraint, at least in the period before the
Lambeth Conference of 1988. It is also accepted that the Lambeth
Conference itself cannot decide the matter and legislate for the

wider Communion. The Report suggests that what is clear in the responses is that preserving and maintaining the unity of the Anglican Communion is the concern of all who responded. Moreover, it was recognised that bishops 'hold the communion together' and therefore any non-recognition of episcopal ministry would inevitably mean an impairing of communion. 'What is hard to bear in regard to the presbyterate would appear to be even more threatening to unity in relation to the episcopate'.

191   The main section of the Grindrod Report explores five issues that any Province would need to have considered before deciding to go ahead and consecrate a woman:

-   is the ordination of women to the threefold order of ministry a legitimate development of the theology and practice of ministry?

-   the episcopal ministry and its relationship to the communion or fellowship of the Church

-   the process of consultation and decision making in the fellowship of the Anglican Communion

-   the process of consultation and decision making when there is division in the universal Church

-   the nature of the Church and of the unity we seek as a credible sign of the Kingdom in a divided world.

192   The Working Party was not asked to make recommendations nor did it. However, in the last chapter the Working Party states that it had been constantly struck by the importance of the theological concept of reception in the process of forming and articulating the mind of the people of God:

The episcopate is not the possession of an individual Province but belongs to the Church. Therefore any decision regarding the fundamental expression of the episcopate would need ultimately to be affirmed by the Church. Those Provinces which are convinced that it is right to consecrate a woman as bishop may wish to exercise restraint because of the possible disruptive effects upon the Communion. Alternatively, they may be persuaded by compelling doctrinal reasons, by their experience of women in ordained ministry and by the demands of the mission of the Church in their region to proceed to the ordination of a woman to the episcopate. This would only be done with overwhelming support in the dioceses concerned. Such a step could only be taken within an over-riding acknowledgement of the need to offer such a development for reception, or indeed rejection, by the whole Communion and by the universal Church and with care and support for the women so ordained.

Were a Province to ordain a woman as bishop:

- The development should be offered to the Anglican Communion in an open process of reception.

- The development could not be expressed as the mind of the Church until it were accepted by the whole Communion. Even then there would necessarily be a tentativeness about it until it were accepted by the universal Church.

- Consideration of the ordination of women to the presbyterate and episcopate within the Communion would need to continue with Provinces listening to one another's thoughts and experiences, aiding one another in theological reflection and exercising mutual sensitivity and care.

- Debate in the wider fellowship of the Churches ought to be encouraged, particularly within existing bilateral and multi-lateral dialogues (37).

(iv) Final Reflections

193   We believe that we identified the main issues relating to women and the episcopate in our earlier report GS 764. As we said there, most of us believe it is difficult to sustain an argument for any essential sacramental distinction between the presbyterate and episcopate such as to put in doubt the possibility of a woman's admission to the episcopate once the presbyterate has been granted. There are some of us, on the grounds of the authority of

jurisdiction which belongs to a bishop and those biblical passages about headship which we looked at in Chapter 3, who are against women being bishops.

194   It is, however, the special role of a bishop as symbol and link of communion between his Church and the universal Church that makes the issue of the consecration of a woman as bishop more difficult than ordination to the presbyterate. As long as some Provinces remain actively opposed to women in the episcopate and their bishops maintain that they could not share collegially with a woman bishop then there is reason for restraint. It is not easy to see how legislation to consecrate women could be drawn up within a Province when some dioceses remain opposed or indeed when Provinces remain opposed. If bishops across the Communion could not recognise each other and were unable to act collegially that would, we believe, be more damaging to communion than the non-recognition of women presbyters. It is possible to legislate diocese by diocese for women priests and to enshrine pastoral guidelines in a code of practice. It is difficult to see how this could be possible in the case of women bishops.

195   In our earlier Report we set out in some detail the relation of the bishops to the communion of the Church. Most of us continue to believe that for this reason it would be difficult were a woman to be consecrated to the episcopate now. However, some of us also acknowledge that many, not only women, view the idea of an all male episcopate as providing an unbalanced group for directing and taking decisions on behalf of the whole Church. The sight of an all male Lambeth Conference at the end of the twentieth century is for some people anachronistic and for some women a sign of disunity rather than unity. This point was made most sharply in the submission to the Grindrod Working Party by the New Zealand House of Bishops:

The Lambeth Conference while respected as a body of
insight and leadership cannot be seen as a
decision-making body on such an issue as the
consecration of women to the episcopate, for not only is
it not representative of those other sections of the
Church, but crucially important on this issue, it is
totally male. New Zealand Anglicans are slowly
beginning to realise, because of their experience, that
it is very unwise for any group of men to attempt to
speak for women, or offer a 'women's point of view' on
anything and this issue is surely one which crucially
requires such a perspective (38).

196 All of us welcome the restraint shown by those Provinces
which have declared their desire to consecrate a woman to the
episcopate. We are grateful for the consultation, sharing of
opinions and listening that has already taken place and which will
continue at the Lambeth Conference. We look forward to further
consultation both during and after the Conference. In particular
some of us believe it important to think more deeply about how we
might remain in communion should one or more Province, decide to
consecrate a woman.

197 There are those of us who cannot see any theological
objections to a woman being consecrated to the episcopate. Others
of us consider that to ordain women to the episcopate, as to the
presbyterate, would be a fundamental change to the Church's
ministry and not a legitimate development. Wherever we stand as
individuals on these matters we are all agreed that to ordain a
woman to the episcopate at this time would certainly be regarded
by many as a break in communion. We all recognise that to imperil
further the unity of the Anglican Communion is a very grave matter
indeed.

Appendix

THE CORRESPONDENCE BETWEEN POPE JOHN PAUL II, THE ARCHBISHOP OF CANTERBURY AND CARDINAL WILLEBRANDS

The Pope to the Archbishop of Canterbury

The long but necessary task of evaluating the Final Report of the first Anglican-Roman Catholic International Commission, in which both our Communions are now engaged, is a vital part of that journey of faith on which we have embarked together in our efforts to reestablish full ecclesial communion. It has been a joy to learn how seriously this task is being taken in so many countries, and how this study is frequently associated with joint action and common witness which express, as far as possible, the degree of communion which has already been brought about between us by the grace of God.

This degree of communion, indeed God's very call to us to be one, also bids us face frankly the differences which still separate us. While the Catholic Church must always be sensitive to the heritage which she has in common with other Christians, she must nevertheless base frank and constructive dialogue upon clarity regarding her own positions.

It was in this spirit that, in an important exchange of letters in 1975-1976, Pope Paul I affirmed to Archbishop Coggan the position of the Catholic Church concerning the admission of women to priestly ordination, a step at that time being considered by several Churches of the Anglican Communion. The reasons that he then stated briefly for the Catholic Church's adherence to the long tradition on this matter were set out at length by the Sacred Congregation for the Doctrine of the Faith in the declaration Inter Insigniores of 15 October 1976. This same position was again stated clearly by observers from the Secretariat for Promoting Christian Unity during the hearing on this subject at the Lambeth Conference of 1978.

I know that Your Grace is well aware of the position of the Catholic Church and of the theological grounds which lead her to maintain it; indeed I am grateful that, in the recent debate in the General Synod of the Church of England, you referred to the implications of this question for Anglican relations with the Catholic and Orthodox Churches. But the outcome of that debate prompts me to reaffirm with all brotherly frankness the continuing adherence of the Catholic Church to the practice and principles so clearly stated by Pope Paul VI.

With his well-known affection for the Anglican Communion and his deep desire for Christian unity, it was with profound sadness that Pope Paul VI contemplated a step which he saw as introducing into our dialogue "an element of grave difficulty", even "a threat". Since that time we have celebrated together the progress towards reconciliation between our two Communions. But in those same years the increase in the number of Anglican Churches which admit, or are preparing to admit, women to priestly ordination constitutes, in the eyes of the Catholic Church, an increasingly serious obstacle to that progress.

Pope Paul VI stated that "obstacles do not destroy mutual commitment to a search for reconciliation". We too were "encouraged by our reliance on the grace of God and by all that we have seen of the power of that grace in the ecumenical movement of our time" when we set up the new Commission, whose task includes study of "all that hinders the mutual recognition of the ministries of our two Communions" (Common Declaration, 29 May 1982, no.3). It is in that same hope, in the charity that "hopes all things" (I Cor 13,7) but which seeks the unity of Christ's Body by "speaking the truth in love" (Eph 4,15), that I write these words to you, my dear Brother, as we celebrate the birth of the Lord who came in "the fulness of time to unite all things" (Eph 1:10).

JOANNES PAULUS II
20th December, 1984

The Archbishop of Canterbury to the Pope

Your Holiness

The Churches of the Anglican Communion and the Roman Catholic Church are fully committed to the quest for full ecclesial unity. No one, however, anticipates that the path towards unity will be without difficulties. One such difficulty, I fully recognise, is the difference of thinking and action about the ordination of women to the ministerial priesthood.

The receipt of your letter of December last year on this question therefore prompted me to confidential consultation with the Primates of the autonomous provinces of the Anglican Communion throughout the world. They also judged your letter to be of great importance and by various means themselves sought the counsel of their own Provinces. Accordingly it is only now that I am able to make a substantive reply to your letter in the light of the responses I have received from the different parts of the Anglican Communion.

Before all else I want to thank Your Holiness for the constructive and frank character or your letter. The question of admission of women to the ministerial priesthood is a divisive matter not only between our Churches but also within them. It is surely a sign of both the seriousness and the maturity of Anglican-Roman Catholic relations that we can exchange letters on a subject surrounded by controversy. I read your letter as an expression of that responsibility in pastoral care for the unity of all God's people which is part of the office of the Bishop of Rome. You may be certain that I received your letter in the same spirit of brotherly love with which it was sent and also intend this reply to reflect that "speaking the truth in love" of which your letter spoke.

In this fraternal spirit I am bound to report that - although Anglican opinion is itself divided - those Churches which have admitted women to priestly ministry have done so for serious doctrinal reasons. I have therefore felt an obligation to explain this more fully in a letter to His Eminence Cardinal Jan Willebrands, President of the Vatican Secretariat for Promoting Christian Unity, whose recent letter to the Co-Chairmen of the Anglican-Roman Catholic International Commission now raises the discussion of the reconciliation of ministries to some prominence in the theological dialogue between our Churches. I fully realise what a serious obstacle the actual admission of women to the priesthood appears to place in the way of such a possibility.

I would therefore propose to Your Holiness the urgent need for a joint study of the question of the ordination of women to the ministerial priesthood, especially in respect of its consequences for the mutual reconciliation of our Churches and the recognition of their ministries. Indeed such a study seems already implicit in the mandate of the Anglican-Roman Catholic International Commission expressed in our Common Declaration at Canterbury of 29 May 1982.

Though the difficulty is grave, to face it together would, I suggest, give real substance to the hopes expressed at the end of your letter. While neither of us can under-estimate the seriousness of this obstacle, I know that we are both convinced that our two Communions ought to maintain the mature trust in each other which has been built up over recent years. Because we have a grave responsibility to continue and intensify our co-operation and dialogue in everything which promotes our growth towards unity, there is a special obligation to tackle such a potentially serious difficulty. In this I believe our two communities will be sustained by their hope and confidence in the Holy Spirit, who alone can bring unity to fulfilment - a fulfilment we need to strive for without wearying and to receive in humility as his gift.

+ROBERT CANTUAR

Archbishop of Canterbury
11 December 1985

The Archbishop of Canterbury to Cardinal Willebrands
Your Eminence

The letter sent to me by His Holiness Pope John Paul II of December last year concerning the question of the admission of women to priestly ordination is one of great importance and weight. I have needed time for reflection and consultation within the Anglican Communion before making a considered and substantive reply. I am deeply conscious that such a letter would not have been written if the Churches of the Anglican Communion and the Roman Catholic Church were not deeply committed to the search for full ecclesial unity and that the far reaching progress already achieved may appear to be checked by the actual admission of women to the priesthood in some Anglican Provinces - and its possibility in others, including the Church of England.

In my letter to the Holy Father I have stated that those Provinces which have acted in this matter have done so for serious doctrinal reasons. I have also said to the Holy Father that I feel an obligation to explain this more fully to you both out of respect for the integrity of those Anglican Provinces which have so acted and because an authentic ecumenical dialogue must be built upon the utmost candour as well as charity. It is my sincere hope that this letter will help the Roman Catholic Church to interpret the opinions and actions of the Churches of the Anglican Communion more intelligibly and sympathetically, while still dissenting from the position of some Anglican Provinces in admitting women to the ministerial priesthood.

In the first place it must be said that the Holy Father's statement of the position of the Roman Catholic Church will clarify the dialogue between our Churches. Those responsible for the dialogue between us will be able to pursue their task more realistically by knowing that the position of the Catholic Church remains the same as it was in the exchange of letters between Pope Paul VI and my predecessor, and more fully set out in the Declaration of the Sacred Congregation of the Faith, Inter Insigniores, of 1976. Ecumenical dialogue must be based on the presentation of the authentic positions of the Churches. While some Roman Catholic theologians may have suggested otherwise to Anglicans, I understand the Holy Father's letter as affirming that the Roman Catholic Church believes that it has no right to change a tradition unbroken throughout the history of the Church, universal in the East and in the West, and considered to be truly Apostolic.

On the Anglican side there has been a growing conviction that there exist in Scripture and Tradition no fundamental objections to the ordination of women to the ministerial priesthood. This

has been expressed synodically by a number of Provinces. Within the internal debate upon this matter - a debate which has developed with growing intensity for over 40 years - Anglicans would generally doubt whether the New Testament by itself alone permits a clear settlement of the issue once and for all.
When we turn to the Tradition of the universal Church, those Anglican Provinces which have proceeded to the ordination of women to the presbyterate have done so with the sincere conviction that the Tradition is open to this development, because the exclusion of women from priestly ministry cannot be proved to be of 'divine law'. Nor have they intended to depart from the traditional understanding of apostolic ministry. Nevertheless, I recognise that in view of the universal Tradition of East and West, it is insufficient simply to state that there are no fundamental reasons against the admission of women to the priesthood. For so significant a theological development it is not enough to assert that there are no reasons against such a proposed action. It is also necessary to demonstrate compelling doctrinal reasons for such a development.

Leaving aside sociological and cultural considerations, as these bear mainly upon the question of whether such ordinations would be opportune, I feel an obligation to report to Your Eminence what I consider to be the most substantial doctrinal reason, which is seen not only to justify the ordination of women to the priesthood by some Anglican Provinces, but actually to require it.

The fundamental principle of the Christian economy of salvation - upon which there is no question of disagreement between Anglicans and Roman Catholics - is that the Eternal Word assumed our human flesh in order that through the Passion, Resurrection and Ascension of the Lord Jesus Christ this same humanity might be redeemed and taken up into the life of the Triune Godhead. In words common to both our liturgical traditions: "As he came to share in our humanity, so we may share in the life of his divinity".

It is also common ground between us that the humanity taken by the Word, and now the risen and ascended humanity of the Lord of all creation, must be a humanity inclusive of women, if half the human race is to share in the Redemption he won for us on the Cross.

Some Anglicans would however then go on to point to the representative nature of the ministerial priesthood. They would argue that priestly character lies precisely in the fact that the priest is commissioned by the Church in ordination to represent the priestly nature of the whole body and also - especially in the presidency of the eucharist - to stand in a special sacramental relationship with Christ as High Priest in whom complete humanity

130

is redeemed and who ever lives to make intercession for us at the right hand of the Father. Because the humanity of Christ our High Priest includes male and female, it is thus urged that the ministerial priesthood should now be opened to women in order the more perfectly to represent Christ's inclusive High Priesthood.

This argument makes no judgement upon the past, but is strengthened today by the fact that the representational nature of the ministerial priesthood is actually weakened by a solely male priesthood, when exclusively male leadership has been largely surrendered in many human societies.

I must also say something of the experience of those Anglican Churches which have taken the step of admitting women to the ministerial priesthood. While honesty compells me to acknowledge deep division on this matter amongst Anglicans - even to the extent of tensions which strain the bonds of communion - those Provinces which have taken this step have indicated to me that their experience has been generally beneficial. Nor have they yet heard compelling arguments to abandon this development. It is also possible that some other Provinces of the Anglican Communion will take similar decisions in their respective Synods.

It is however by no means a foregone conclusion that the General Synod of the Church of England will immediately move in such a direction, for it is not yet clear whether a sufficient consensus has been reached to effect the proposals called for by the Synod last November which prompted the Holy Father's letter. Other Anglican Provinces have also indicated to me that they are unlikely to ordain women in the immediate future. While Anglican diversity of opinion and practice must be a difficulty for the Roman Catholic Church, I believe it is also an indication of the fact that Anglicans are still seeking the will of God in this matter. Nor can this be discovered by either of our Churches without the wider, general study and experience of the role of women in the community of the Church. In this context the admission of women to the diaconate in Anglican Churches is important, as is the ministry of women religious within the Roman Catholic Church.

As you already know, I am not myself convinced that action should be taken on ordination to the presbyterate by Anglicans alone, no matter how convincing the positive arguments, until there is a wider consensus in our Churches. I believe the argument for ecumenical restraint is also a doctrinal one because it is only in such a wider perspective that particular churches can truly discern the mind of the whole Church.

At the same time realism, together with an acquaintance with the history of the Church, prompts me to recall that until such time as Christians have clearly discerned the mind of the church in matters of contention, there has often arisen sharp discussion, debate and even conflict. It is indeed through such conflict and debate that the truth is often discerned. You will already know that the question of the ordination of women to the priesthood is the occasion of such sharp debate within the Anglican Communion at the present time. I also recognise that this development appears to be a serious obstacle to the eventual reconciliation of our churches and have expressed this in my letter to the Holy Father.

It is at such difficult times that dialogue is essential. This is especially necessary in the light of the increasingly close relationship which has developed betweeen the Churches of the Anglican Communion and the Roman Catholic Church in many parts of the world and in view of the crucial stage we are reaching as we engage in the task of evaluating the Final Report of the first Anglican-Roman Catholic International Commission. It is also urgent in the light of the constructive letter you have sent to the Co-Chairmen of the ARCIC on the question of the reconciliation of ministries. I believe that letter provides the proper context for the dialogue I have proposed to the Holy Father. As the International Commission cannot fail to have to examine the ordination of women if it is to fulfil its mandate "to study all that hinders the mutual recognition of the ministries of our Communions" (Common Declaration, 29 May 1982), I also believe the Commission will be the right forum for this difficult discussion. Having said this it may be that we should envisage the possibility of some strengthening of the Commission by the addition of special consultants for this particular task.

Your Eminence will know that the writing of my letters to the Holy Father and yourself has been no light matter. When sister Churches have been estranged for 400 years, but at last begin to see tangible signs of reconciliation, it is particularly painful to find this new obstacle between us. But in writing this fuller letter to you I have been helped by our personal friendship and by my absolute confidence in your sympathetic understanding of the Anglican position. I hope I have been able to express my consciousness of the reasons why the Roman Catholic Church finds itself unable to accept the ordination of women to the priesthood.

Though we do not see the way forward from what at present appears to be mutually incompatible positions - at least where some Anglican Provinces have actually ordained women to the priesthood - I am given hope by the fact that those who began the doctrinal dialogue between us 20 years ago did not themselves see the end from the beginning. May the same Holy Spirit which assisted them in the search for agreement in faith, and whose Report both Churches are in the process of evaluating and receiving, also assist their successors who will, should the Holy Father be in agreement with my proposal, have the weighty responsibility for seeking a way forward.

+ROBERT CANTUAR

Archbishop of Canterbury
18 December 1985

Cardinal Willebrands to the Archbishop of Canterbury

Your Grace

I thank you most sincerely for your letter of 22 November 1985 on the question of the ordination of women. Especially I thank you for setting out so clearly the reasons why those provinces of the Anglican Communion which have proceeded to ordain women to the priesthood feel justified in so doing. I acknowledge that your letter is the fruit both of considerable reflection on your part and of consultation with the Primates of the Anglican Communion. That this matter has been taken up so seriously is a measure of the confidence that exists between us and of the progress that has been made to overcome the divisions between Anglicans and Roman Catholics. It will be especially important for those who have the task of continuing the dialogue between our Communions to understand the theological reasons why some in the Anglican Communion see the ordination of women to be justified and even required. It is equally important that something be said about the mind of the Catholic Church in relation to the ideas and arguments set out in your letter.

My purpose in this reply is not to enter in an exhaustive analysis of the questions which this problem raises. I agree with you that this issue cannot fail to arise on the agenda of the second Anglican-Roman Catholic International Commission which has the task of studying all those things which stand in the way of mutual recognition of each other's ministries. It is in that context and in that perspective that I too would envisage further study and reflection on this question taking place.

What I would like to do is to refer to some specific points made in your letter and I wish first of all to speak to a point you make towards the end of your letter. You say that you yourself are not convinced that Anglicans should go ahead with the ordination of women "until there is a wider consensus in our Churches". This observation seems to me to open up a profound theological dimension of this question. The ordination only of men to the presbyterate and episcopate is the unbroken Tradition of the Catholic and Orthodox Churches. Neither Church understands itself to be competent to alter this Tradition. In 1976, the Congregation for the Doctrine of the Faith, in the declaration Inter Insigniores, stated clearly that "the Catholic Church does not consider herself to be authorised to admit women to priestly ordination". The principal reason put forward in the declaration was that of Tradition (cf. Inter Ins. I-IV). The constant Tradition of the Catholic and Orthodox Churches has considered the practice of Christ and the Apostles as a norm from which she could not deviate. The practice of the Church to ordain only men embodies her fidelity under the guidance of the Holy Spirit to what was given by Christ. The declaration, together with the earlier correspondence on the subject between Pope Paul VI and Archbishop Coggan, is where Catholics must look for guidance.

I am aware that some of those in the Anglican Communion who oppose the ordination of women give as their reasons that since the Anglican Communion is part of the whole Catholic Church, it cannot undertake so radical a departure from Tradition independently of the Roman Catholic and Orthodox Churches. The Anglican Communion, on this view, cannot act alone and may not prescind from the practice and understanding of the wider Church. I propose that this point of view merits serious reflection. The Catholic Church takes very seriously the considerable progress that has been made towards our eventual goal of full communion of faith and sacramental life. Our greater unity must be a fundamental concern, and it has to be stated frankly that a development like the ordination of women does nothing to deepen the communion between us and weakens the communion that currently exists. The ecclesiological implications are serious.

Having said this, I take very seriously your point that those in the Anglican Communion who have proceeded to the ordination of women have only felt able to do so on the basis of serious theological conviction. This I welcome, since it must be clearly stated that this is a theological issue and cannot be resolved on sociological or cultural grounds. The question of the rights of women to hold secular office is a quite separate matter and should not in any way be connected or paralleled with the question of women's ordination. The context for that discussion is the context of sacramental theology and the tradition of the Church. My comments will, I trust, illustrate this point.

I have given considerable thought to the theological arguments for the ordination of women which you report. As I have said, I do not propose to deal in detail with this question, but I do wish to indicate why I consider these arguments to be unsatisfactory.

If I understand it correctly, the thrust of the argument is this: Christ is our High Priest. The humanity he assumed to accomplish our redemption was a humanity that included both male and female. That is to say, his humanity must be understood as an inclusive humanity, if the whole human race is to be able to enjoy the fruits of the redemption. Those who are commissioned as priests in the Church fulfil a twofold representative function: not only do they represent the priestly nature of the whole body of the Church, they also stand in a special sacramental relationship with the risen Christ. Especially in the Eucharist, they represent Christ. Since Christ's humanity is inclusive of male and female, those who represent Christ in the Church would do so more perfectly if their number included both males and females.

My first observation would be to note that the language used in this argumentation is the language of priesthood and sacrament. This makes it clear that what is at issue is precisely the question of sacramental ordination of women to ministerial priesthood. It is important to draw attention to this, so as to make clear that this discussion is directly relevant only to those Christians who share this understanding of Christian ministry. For our two communions, the stimulus to our present correspondence is the Final Report of the Anglican-Roman Catholic International Commission (ARCIC-I). That Commission claimed to have reached substantial agreement on the doctrine of ministry. So we are addressing a problem that arises in the context of real progress being made towards a common mind on the sacramental nature of ministry. In addressing this issue now, I write as one for whom the sacramental understanding of the ministry is part of the faith of the Church. The issue then, is the ordination of women to the priesthood and, that being so, it is clear that the question of who can or cannot be ordained may not be separated from its appropriate context of sacramental theology and ecclesiology. The practice of only ordaining men to the priesthood has to be seen in the context of ecclesiology in which the priesthood is an integral and essential aspect of the reality of the Church. It is in and through the ministry of priests that the once-for-all sacrifice of Christ is present reality. So there is real continuity between the redemptive work of Christ and the priestly office exercised both by those in the episcopal order and by their collaborators in the order of presbyters.

I do acknowledge and welcome the fact that the arguments for the ordination of women which you report are clearly arguments of those who believe deeply in the important place of the ordained ministry in God's economy of salvation. But what I must seriously question is whether they constitute an adequate or proper understanding of that economy of salvation as revealed in the Scriptures and meditated and preached in the Church. I will give the indications of why I say this.

The picture of human redemption that is now before us in the Scriptures is of a God who is powerful to save and of a people who receive salvation as a free gift. Feminine imagery is used to reveal the place of the human family in God's plan of salvation. In the Old Testament, the people of Israel is depicted as the bride of Yahweh. In the New Testament St Paul speaks of the Church as the bride of Christ. In its tradition, the Church has understood itself in terms of this feminine imagery and symbolism as the Body which received the Word of God, and which is fruitful in virtue of that which has been received. Mary, the Mother of God, is, in her response to the Word of God, a type of the Church. Christ, on the other hand, is the Head of the Body, and it is through the Head that the whole Body is redeemed. It is precisely in this perspective that the representative role of the ministerial priesthood is to be understood.

Christ took on human nature to accomplish the redemption of all humanity. But as Inter Insigniores says, "we can never ignore the fact that Christ is a man". His male identity is an inherent feature of the economy of salvation, revealed in the Scriptures and pondered in the Church. The ordination only of men to the priesthood has to be understood in terms of the intimate relationship between Christ the redeemer and those who, in a unique way, cooperate in Christ's redemptive work. The priest represents Christ in His saving relationship with His Body the Church. He does not primarily represent the priesthood of the whole People of God. However unworthy, the priest stands in persona Christi. Christ's saving sacrifice is made present in the world as a sacramental reality in and through the ministry of priests. And the sacramental ordination of men takes on force and significance precisely within this context of the Church's experience of its own identity, of the power and significance of the person of Jesus Christ, and of the symbolic and iconic role of those who represent him in the Eucharist.

In saying this I wish simply to make the point that the arguments you relay on cannot count as reasons for the radical innovation of ordaining women to the priesthood; the arguments do not negotiate the manifold theological issues which this matter raises. The possible future consequences of introducing such a practice at this point of time also require careful attention. This topic will, of course, continue to be a matter of discussion and in the context of the Anglican-Roman Catholic dialogue the most immediate question will be about how the ordination of women in some parts of the Anglican Communion affects progress towards fuller communion between us. We may not doubt that, under the power and inspiration of God, whose ways are not our ways, and whose thoughts are not our thoughts, those deliberations will contribute towards the unity for which Christ prayed.

+JOHANNES CARDINAL WILLEBRANDS

17 June 1986

REFERENCES

1. The Ordination of Women to the Priesthood. A Consultative Document presented by the Advisory Council for the Church's Ministry, GS 104, CIO, 1972.

The Ordination of Women to the Priesthood. A Supplement to the Consultative Document GS 104, CIO, 1978.

The Ordination of Women to the Priesthood: Further Report. A Background paper by Christian Howard, GS Misc 198, CIO, 1984.

2. Santer, H.,'Stereotyping the Sexes in Society and in the Church', Feminine in the Church, ed. M. Furlong, SPCK, 1984, p.146.

3. The Ordination of Women to the Priesthood: A Report by the House of Bishops, GS 764, 1987, para. 8.

4. Lampe, G.W.H., 'Women and the Ministry of Priesthood', Explorations in Theology, 8, 1981. p.97.

5. Declaration on the Question of the Admission of Women to Ministerial Priesthood: Inter Insigniores, CTS, London, 1977.

6. Rousseau, M., in The Way, Vol. 21, No.3, 1981, p.214.

7. Gregory Nazianzen, Epist. Ad Cledonium, J.P. Migne, Patrologia Graeca XXXVII, 181C.

8. Norris, R.A., 'The Ordination of Women and the "Maleness" of the Christ', Feminine in the Church, ed. M. Furlong, SPCK, 1984, p.76.

9. We Believe in God, Report of the Doctrine Commission of the Church of England, Church House Publishing, 1987, p.58.

10. Santer, H., op. cit., p.148.

11. Augustine, On the Holy Trinity, quoted in Julia O'Faolain and Laura Martines, Not in God's Image, Virago, 1979, p.97.

12. The Priesthood of the Ordained Ministry, GS 694, Church House Publishing, 1986, para. 147.

13. cf: Women and the Episcopate Report of the Working Party appointed by the Primates of the Anglican Communion, ACC, 1987.

14. Baptism, Eucharist and Ministry, Faith and Order Paper 111, WCC, Geneva, 1982.

15. cf Appendix.

16. God's Reign and Our Unity, The Report of the Anglican-Reformed International Commission, SPCK, 1984, para. 104.

17. Women and the Episcopate, para. 11.

18. The Nature of Christian Belief: A Statement and Exposition by the House of Bishops of the General Synod of the Church of England, Church House Publishing, 1986, para 12.

19. We Believe in God, Report of the Doctrine Commission, Church House Publishing, 1987, Chapter 1.

20. ibid.

21. ibid.

22. The Nature of Christian Belief, footnote, p.8.

23. ibid.

24. We Believe in God Chapter 1.

25. Servants of the Lord, GS Misc 224

26. Slee, N., 'Parables and Women's Experience', The Modern Churchman, XXVI, 2, 1985.

27. Tanner, M., 'Called to Priesthood: Interpreting Women's Experience', Feminine in the Church, ed. M. Furlong, SPCK, 1984, pp 150ff.

28. cf Appendix

29. Women and the Episcopate, paras 10-45.

30. Williams, R., 'Women and the Ministry: A Case for Theological Seriousness', Feminine in the Church, ed. M. Furlong, SPCK, 1984, p21.

31. Report of the United and Uniting Churches, WCC, 1987.

32. cf Appendix

33. The Lambeth Conference 1978.

34. 'Authority II', para 25, The Final Report of the Anglican Roman Catholic International Commission, CTS/SPCK, 1982.

35. Gathered for Life: The Official Report of the Vancouver Assembly, WCC, 1983.

36. Women and the Episcopate para. 2.

37. ibid., para. 94.

38. ibid., para. 24.

BIBLIOGRAPHY OF SYNOD PAPERS

Women and Holy Orders, Report of the Archbishops' Commission, CIO, 1966. This Report contains an extensive bibliography (pp. 40-44) of the relevant material to date.

Women in Ministry: a Study, CIO, 1968, Report of a Working Party set up jointly by the Council for Women's Ministry in the Church and the Ministry Committee of ACCM.

The Ordination of Women to the Priesthood, A Consultative Document presented by the Advisory Council for the Church's Ministry, GS 104, CIO, 1972.

The Ordination of Women to the Priesthood, A Supplement to the Consultative Document GS 104, CIO, 1978.

The Ordination of Women to the Priesthood: Further Report, A Background Paper by Christian Howard, GS Misc 198, CIO, 1984.

The Priesthood of the Ordained Ministry, GS 694, BMU/Church House Publishing 1986, Chapter XI

The Ordination of Women to the Priesthood: The Scope of the Legislation, GS 738, 1986.

The Ordination of Women to the Priesthood, A Report by the House of Bishops, GS 764, 1987.